Dale J. Sieverding

The Reception of Baptized Christians: A History and Evaluation

Liturgy Training Publications
in cooperation with

The North American Forum
on the Catechumenate

Acknowledgments

The Forum Essay series is a cooperative effort of The North American Forum on the Catechumenate and Liturgy Training Publications. The purpose of the series is to provide a forum for exploring issues emerging from the implementation of the order of Christian initiation and from the renewal of the practice of reconciliation in the Roman Catholic Church.

Other titles in the series:

The Role of the Assembly in Christian Initiation
    Catherine Vincie, RSHM
Eucharist as Sacrament of Initiation
    Nathan D. Mitchell
On the Rite of Election
    Rita Ferrone
Preaching the Rites of Christian Initiation
    Jan Michael Joncas
Liturgical Spirituality and the Rite of Christian Initiation of Adults
    Shawn Madigan
Images of Baptism
    Maxwell E. Johnson

THE RECEPTION OF BAPTIZED CHRISTIANS: A HISTORY AND EVALUATION © 2001 Archdiocese of Chicago: Liturgy Training Publications, 1800 North Hermitage Avenue, Chicago IL 60622-1101; 1-800-933-1800, fax 1-800-933-7094, e-mail orders@ltp.org. All rights reserved. See our website at www.ltp.org.

All scripture citations are taken from the *New Revised Standard Version* Bible, © 1989, Division of Christian Education of the National Council of Churches of Christ in the United States of America.

This *Forum Essay* was designed by Mary Bowers and typeset in Frutiger and Bembo by Jim Mellody-Pizzato. The cover design is by Barb Rohm. Carol Mycio was the production editor. Printed by Printing Arts Chicago in Cicero, Illinois. Editors for the series are Victoria M. Tufano (Liturgy Training Publications) and Jim Schellman (The North American Forum on the Catechumenate).

07   06   05   04   03   02   01   5   4   3   2   1

Library of Congress Control Number: 2001091625

ISBN 1-56854-175-9
RECBAP

Contents

■

■

Abbreviations

AAS	*Acta Apostolicae Sedis.*
ACC	Alcuin Club Collection, London.
Acta et documenta: Antepraeparatoria	*Acta et documenta Concilio Oecumenico Vaticano II apparando,* Series I, 4 volumes (15 parts). Antepraeparatoria. Vatican City 1960–1961.
Acta et documenta: Praeparatoria	*Acta et documenta Concilio Oecumenico Vaticano II apparando,* Series II, 3 volumes (7 parts). Praeparatoria. Vatican City 1964–1969.
ANF	*Ante-Nicene Fathers,* Grand Rapids.
Acta Synodalia	*Acta Synodalia Sacrosancti Concilii Oecumenici Vaticani II,* 5 volumes (27 parts), Vatican City 1970–1990.
ACW	Ancient Christian Writers, Mahwah, NJ/New York.
CCL	*Corpus Christianorum, Series Latina,* Turnhout, Belgium.
CSEL	*Corpus scriptorum ecclesiasticorum latinorum,* Vienna.
DOL	*Documents on the Liturgy 1963–1979: Conciliar, Papal and Curial Texts,* (ed. T. O'Brien) Collegeville, 1982. All citations are noted according to the paragraph designation in the margins unless otherwise noted by page number.
DS	Denzinger, H. and Schönmetzer, A., *Enchiridion Symbolorum definitionum et declarationum de rebus fidei et morum,* Rome: Herder, 1975, 36th edition.
DSE	Denzinger, H., (trans. R. Deferrari), *The Sources of Catholic Dogma* (trans. of *Enchridion Symbolorum,* 1954, 30th edition) London 1957.
EEC	*Encyclopedia of the Early Church,* Cambridge 1992.
EL	*Ephemerides Liturgicae,* Rome.
FOC	*The Fathers of the Church,* Washington, D.C.
GeV	*Sacramentarium Gelasianum vetus.*
MoO	*Liber Ordinum.*
MR	*Missale Romanum 1970/5.*
OICA	*Rituale Romanum ex decreto Sacrosancti Oecumenici Concilii Vaticani II instauratum auctoritate pauli PP. VI promulgatum, Ordo initiationis christianae adultorum, editio typica* Vatican City 1972, (reimpressio emendata) 1974.

OR	M. Andrieu, *Les Ordines Romani du haut moyen-âge, V Tomes,* Spicilegium Sacrum Lovaniense 11, 23, 24, 28, Louvain 1931–1961.
PL	*Patrologia Latina,* Migne.
PR 1595/6	*Pontificale Romanum Clementis VIII P.M. iussu restitutum atque editum,* Rome 1595.
PR 1595/1848	*Pontificale Romanum, Summorum Pontificium iussu editum et a Benedicto XIV Pont. Max. recognitum et castigatum,* Rome 1848.
PRG-X	C. Vogel and R. Elze, *Le Pontifical Romano-Germanique du dixième siècle,* III tomes, *Studi e Testi* 226, 227, 269, Vatican City 1963–1972.
PR-XIII	M. Andrieu, *Le Pontifical romain au moyen-âge,* Tome II: Le Pontifical de la Curie Romaine au XIIIe siècle, *Studi e Testi* 87, Vatican City 1940 (reprint 1984).
PGD	M. Andrieu, *Le Pontifical romain au moyen-âge,* Tome III, *Le Pontifical de Guillaume Durand, Studi e Testi* 88, Vatican City 1940 (reprint 1984).
RCIA-USA 1988	*The Roman Ritual Revised by Decree of the Second Vatican Ecumenical Council and Published by Authority of Pope Paul VI, Rite of Christian Initiation of Adults, Approved for use in the Dioceses of the United States of America by the National Conference of Catholic Bishops and Confirmed by the Apostolic See,* New York 1988.
RR 1614	*Rituale Romanum Pauli V Pont. Max, iussu editum,* Rome 1614.
RR 1614/1952	*Rituale Romanum 1614 Pauli V Pont. Max. iussu editum aliorumque pont. cura recognitum atque ad normam codicis juris canonici accommodatum,* Rome 1952.
SC	*Sources Chrétiennes,* eds. H. de Lubac and J. Daniélou, Paris.
SP	Studia Patristica.
Tanner	*Decrees of the Ecumenical Councils,* 2 vols., (ed. N. Tanner), London 1990.

Introduction

■

The Rite of Reception of Baptized Christians into the Full Communion of the Catholic Church *(Ordo admissionis valide iam baptizatorum in plenam communionem ecclesiae catholicae)*[1] is a new ritual drawn up by the Consilium *(Consilium ad exsequendam constitutionem de Sacra Liturgia)* after the Second Vatican Council. This book seeks to study the ritual and the history of its development. A historical investigation will examine the reception and/or reconciliation of the validly baptized into the communion of the Catholic church. While there are several significant studies on the issue of the reconciliation of heretics done in this century, none of them treat the present liturgy of reception since the most recent study was completed before Vatican II. Two of the studies are canon law dissertations.[2] The other studies are liturgical/sacramental in nature.[3] A recent book offers a short historical treatment of the question with suggestions for the pastoral use of the *ordo*.[4]

In the pastoral situation of the Catholic church in the United States of America, this *ordo* is used often. The majority of persons coming to the Catholic church in the United States have been validly baptized in other churches, thus the rites of the catechumenate are not to be celebrated with them.[5] My interest in the topic comes from pastoral experience of directing the formation process for those preparing for the sacraments of Christian initiation and those preparing for reception into the full communion of the Catholic church.

The *Ordo admissionis* was published as an appendix to the *Rite of Christian Initiation of Adults [Ordo initiationis christianae adultorum (OICA)]*. Numerous theses have been written on the OICA, yet none have treated in depth the topic of ritual of reception into full communion.

The proposal for this book is modest—a historical study of the ritual for the reception of the validly baptized into the full communion of the Catholic church. The study is limited to a treatment of the Western, Latin tradition. It is primarily a liturgical study. It does not pretend to be a work in sacramental theology; thus, there are important related questions such as the validity of baptism (outside the church) and the validity of sacraments (outside the church). These questions will be dealt with only insofar as they impact the understanding of the church's *ritual* practice on the issue. Ecclesiological and canonical questions, such as the position of those baptized outside the church and their relationship to the Catholic church, are also important issues, but outside the scope of the study. Studies already done on these issues will, of course, be noted. There are related issues such as the development of canonical penance and the development of confirmation/chrismation which, while related to the issue, are not the direct goal of this study. These issues will only be treated insofar as they illustrate the church's attitude (ritual and/or pastoral) toward the validly (if heretically) baptized.

Chapter 1 peruses the patristic period, more specifically the Latin tradition. The study offers some definitions of terms before presenting the writing of Tertullian. The chapter then enters into a discussion of the unique situation of the Roman church in the first part of the third century. The main sections of the chapter deal with the aftermath of the Decian persecution and the (re)baptism controversy between the North African and Roman churches. The fourth-century ecumenical councils, as well as some local councils, are presented along with the significant writings of the fathers to the time of Gregory the Great (d. 604).

The second chapter will look at the Western medieval liturgical books. The orations and (where available) rubrics for the reconciliation of heretics are presented. Roman and Gallican sacramentaries are studied as well as two examples from the Visigothic (Mozarabic) tradition. The various rituals *(ordines)* for the reconciliation of those baptized in heresy and/or schism from the medieval pontificals are then examined. Chapter 3 enters into the modern history of the reception into full communion (i.e., the liturgical history immediately prior to Vatican II). This comprises a study of the Tridentine canons on the validity of baptism and an examination of the liturgical books issued following the Council of Trent and other ecclesiastical documents that figure in the reception of converts. Special attention is given to the particular legislation for the church in the United States of America on (re)baptism and reception. The chapter presents the situation of the reception of converts as it was on the eve of the Second Vatican Council.

The drawing up of the new *ordo* for the reception of converts is a direct result of the promulgation of the Constitution on the Sacred Liturgy *(Sacrosanctum concilium):*

> [A] new rite is to be drawn up for converts who have already been validly baptized. It should indicate that they are now admitted to communion with the Church[6]

Chapter 4 delves into the work of the bishops at Vatican II in the development of this paragraph of *Sacrosanctum concilium*. The study includes a look at the first suggestions of the fathers in the ante-preparatory period, the preparatory discussion of the Central Preparatory Commission for the Ecumenical Council and the actual floor discussion of the Council. In addition to this investigation, three other conciliar documents are briefly treated as they had some influence on the formation of the new *ordo*. The First Ecumenical Directory, promulgated in 1967, is presented, for it too had an influence on the formation of the *ordo*.

Chapter 5 begins with a brief look at the documents issued after the *Constitution on the Sacred Liturgy* was promulgated by Pope Paul VI and the bishops. The main part of the chapter is a detailed analysis of the schemata of the Consilium. The examination will follow the progress of the new ritual *(ordo)* from the "discussion of principles" stage to the publication of the Latin typical edition *(editio typica)* in 1972. In the course of the research, where possible, the study will attempt to uncover the methods, the motivations, the intentions and other factors that were influential in drawing up the *ordo*.

The final chapter presents the *Rite of Reception (Ordo admissionis)* as it appears in the liturgical books for use in the United States of America (i.e., the National Statutes on the Catechumenate are treated as well as the adaptations made for celebration of the *ordo* in the USA). The second part of the chapter is a critical evaluation of the *ordo* and its adaptation based on insights from the historical investigation. An attempt will be made to evaluate the *ordo* based on the weight of the tradition, and in light of the goals of the liturgical reform as stated in *Sacrosanctum concilium*, 50 and 62.[7] The essential ritual elements for admission to full communion discovered in the historical treatment will be used as a guide in analyzing the new *ordo* and its adaptations. Finally, suggestions will be offered based on this investigation and analysis for future work on the *Ordo admissionis.*

The study is aided by access to Consilium archives graciously made available by the Congregation for Divine Worship and the Discipline of the Sacraments, the archives of the International Commission on English in the Liturgy, and the archives of the Bishops' Committee on the Liturgy of the National Conference of Catholic Bishops (USA). The correspondence of one consultor (Msgr. Frederick McManus) from the Consilium study group was also available for the study. The intention of this endeavor is to offer not only historical insight into the present *ordo,* but also suggestions for consideration should it be revised in the future.

Chapter I

The Patristic Period

■

In the patristic period, the first Latin writer to have mentioned the issue of baptism outside the church was Tertullian. A native of Carthage in North Africa, Tertullian took a hard line on anyone baptized outside the church's boundaries: "Heretics, have no fellowship in our discipline. . . . [T]hey and we have not the same God, nor the same Christ. Therefore their baptism is not one with ours either" (*De baptismo* XV). According to Tertullian, the Holy Spirit was present in baptism, and since by definition no heretic could be in possession of the Spirit, a baptism administered by a heretic or a person in mortal sin could have no value. One who had received baptism from such a person must be baptized again before being admitted to the one church. His position seems to have been adopted in North Africa as early as 220 CE by Bishop Agrippinus of Carthage. Witness of this is given in the letters of Cyprian of Carthage. The North African church's position can be characterized by this rigorism that would affect its behavior for many years into the future.

The Roman church witnesses a more relaxed attitude toward the reconciliation of penitents. This more welcoming approach was evident in their treatment of those baptized outside the church's communion. Pope Callistus (d. 222) granted reconciliation to sinners. Callistus saw the church as "the home and school of sinners, not as a gathered congregation of saints."[1] It is probable that some churches in communion with Callistus did rebaptize, but the ancient tradition is that it is unlawful to rebaptize.[2]

The Rebaptism Controversy

The first major crisis in the Latin church over rebaptism occurred between Pope Stephen I and Bishop Cyprian of Carthage in the mid-third century. This followed the Decian persecution (beginning in 248) during which many forsook their Christian faith and sacrificed to the gods of the Roman religion, following the order of the emperor. Cyprian took a hard line against those who had sacrificed to the Roman gods, insisting that they be rebaptized on their return to the communion with the church. In Rome a further complication arises: Novatian, a presbyter, broke with the church over the election of Pope Cornelius in 251 and had himself ordained bishop. Novatian took a rigorist position, insisting that anyone coming into communion with his group must be rebaptized.

The period from 250 to the death of Cyprian in 258 saw a great crisis over the issue of baptism outside the church's communion. This is known as the "rebaptism controversy," and it rocked the Latin church. From written testimony, mostly the letters of St. Cyprian, the kernel of the debate can be gleaned. Cyprian saw the church as a tight communion. The acceptance of those baptized by heretics or schismatics endangered the purity of the church. Furthermore, he reasoned, the Spirit could not work outside the church; therefore, heretics, who didn't have the Holy Spirit, could not give that Spirit to those whom they baptized. "[N]o one can be baptized outside and away from the church, on the grounds that there is only one baptism that has been appointed and that is in the holy church."[3] He is quite clear: The heretics coming to the church are not being *rebaptized;* they are being *baptized* because they were never baptized in the first place.[4] Cyprian here distinguishes two groups. The apostates, those who had forsaken the faith and were returning to the church *(ad veritatem et matricem redeant)* are to have hands imposed on them in penance; the heretically baptized are to be washed in the waters of baptism.[5]

Pope Stephen (254–257) held a position completely contrary to Cyprian's. Unfortunately, none of his writings have survived, so his position must be studied from the letters of Cyprian. Stephen declared that baptism given by heretics was valid, so they should not be rebaptized when they come into communion with the church. He claims to have received this tradition from the apostles.[6] Stephen further states that those coming to the church, having been baptized by heretical ministers, need to have hands imposed on them in penance, for the reception of the Holy Spirit.[7]

The gesture of imposing hands in the reception of the heretically baptized was a point of contention. Cyprian saw this imposition as "the second part of the baptismal ritual by which the Holy Spirit was conferred upon a convert baptized outside the church. On this basis, he demonstrated that the practice was incoherent, since the presence of the Spirit was equally necessary for the first part of the ritual, the washing to purify from sin."[8] According to Cyprian, the imposition of hands could reconcile those who had been baptized originally in the communion, left it, and then wished to return. Stephen insisted that the power of the name of Jesus invoked in baptism was enough for efficacy.[9] The imposition of hands *in penance* included the conferral of the Holy Spirit.

Fourth Century

In the fourth century, division again rocked the North African church with the Donatist schism. Several councils in the West and the two ecumenical councils upheld the validity of baptism outside the church's communion. The Council of Arles (314) decreed

> Concerning the Africans, because they use their own law so as to rebaptize, it has been decided that, if anyone from a heretical sect come to the church, he should be asked his creed, and if it is perceived that he has been baptized in the Father and the Son and the Holy Spirit, *only the hand should be imposed upon him, in order that he may receive the Holy Spirit.* But if upon being questioned he does not answer this Trinity, let him be baptized.[10]

This was the position proposed by the Roman church in the mid-third century, and it was adopted at Arles by the bishops of the West.

The ecumenical Council of Nicea (325) speaks about the problem of heretical baptism in two canons (9, 19). Canon 9 speaks about the reception of the Novatians, and says nothing about their rebaptism, implying that they were not baptized upon their reception.[11] Another heretical group, the Paulianists, is dealt with in canon 19. Evidently, they were not baptized in the name of the Trinity, so upon their reception were (re)baptized.[12] The bishops at Nicea distinguished clearly between valid and invalid baptism.

The Council of Laodicea, a local synod of bishops, meeting sometime between 343 and 381, treats the reception of the heretically baptized. Canon 7 of this council requires a renunciation of heresies, followed by a profession of faith and an anointing with holy chrism for certain groups.[13] Canon 8 deals with a group needing to be baptized for reception into the church's communion.[14] The Council of Constantinople (381) treats the reception of the heretically baptized in canon 7. Although the formula and complex anointing that are described in this canon can, through historical studies, be dated from the century after the council itself, they are preserved among the council's canons.[15]

Pope Siricius I (384–398) wrote to a bishop in Spain that heretics are to be reconciled "through the sole invocation of the seven-fold Spirit by the imposition of a bishop's hand."[16] He notes that this was determined in the Synod of East and West. Rebaptism is strongly prohibited also in his letter (calling on the church's long tradition against this practice). The magisterial pronouncement here seems to indicate that for a long time already heretics had been received with the imposition of hands and the invocation of the Holy Spirit.

Later Patristic Era

In the fifth century, a number of popes will again reiterate the Roman church's position in response to queries from local bishops.[17] St. Augustine develops the theology of baptism in his voluminous corpus of writings: Baptism belongs to Christ, and no matter who ministers the baptism, it is still Christ's; therefore, if water is used with the proper (i.e., Trinitarian) invocation, the baptism is valid and cannot be repeated.[18] He witnesses that it is the imposition of hands that is given to the reformed heretic thus bestowing the gift of the Spirit.[19]

Pope Innocent I (401–417) reiterates the tradition of the church, using an interesting phrase: The baptized heretic is received *"under the symbol of penance and the sanctification of the Holy Spirit through the imposition of hands.*[20] A study of this phrase indicates that the imposition of hands in this case is not to be confused with the imposition of hands in canonical penance.[21] Innocent I and Roman bishops in this time make no mention of a chrismation for the reconciliation of heretics. The Holy Spirit is conferred with the imposition of hands. Leo the Great (440–461) uses similar images. He calls only for the sanctification of the Holy Spirit to be invoked over the validly baptized *(sola sanctificatio Spiritus sancti invocanda est).*[22] In a subsequent letter he writes, "If it has been established that people were baptized by heretics, in no way will the sacrament of regeneration be repeated for them. But only that may be conferred which was absent there — that they may gain the strength of the Holy Spirit *through the episcopal imposition of the hands.*"[23]

One writer from southern Gaul, Gennadius of Marseilles (c. 490), notes that an imposition of the hand is given for some heretics while others require an imposition of hands with chrismation. Gregory of Tours (573–594) and Idelfonsus of Toledo (657–669) write about a similar tradition. Contemporary documents from Gallican councils speak of the two actions as well. Experts in the study of this period of Gallican history indicate that the *imposition of hands* and *chrismation* come to be used interchangeably, whether for the post-baptismal rite or for the reception of the heretically baptized.[24] For the patristic era, the reception of those baptized outside the church could be summed up with the pronouncement of Pope Gregory the Great (590–604) in a letter to the bishops of Spain:

> We have taught from the ancient institution of the Fathers that those who are baptized in a heresy in the name of the Trinity, if they return to the holy church, may be recalled to the womb of mother church *either by the anointing of chrism, or by the imposition of the hand or by a mere profession of faith.* For this reason, the West restores Arians to the door of the catholic church through the imposition of the hand, but the East through the anointing of sacred chrism.

But the church receives Monophysites and others by a simple profession of faith because it accepts in them the holy baptism of cleansing, which they once pursued with the heretics. So either the former will have received the Holy Spirit through the imposition of the hand, or the latter will have been united to the heart of the holy and universal church through the profession of the true faith.[25]

Thus we have seen that in the time of St. Gregory the church knows three different ways to receive the validly baptized into communion.

Summation

To evaluate the evidence from the patristic period, the material will be organized under penitential and initiation aspects. It is also important to distinguish between the Roman and Gallican tradition. This summation will attempt to speak to the question of what was the essential element for the reconciliation of heretics.

Penitential Aspects

There are a number of texts from the patristic period that refer to the reconciliation of heretics in terms of penance. Penance was prescribed for the "true apostate; that is, someone baptized in the Catholic church who later lapsed and subsequently wished to return." This is reiterated by many prominent ecclesiastical figures, beginning with Cyprian.[26]

The question becomes much more complicated when we look at the texts applied to the heretically baptized. Pope Stephen uses penitential imagery when he says that people are received through the imposition of hands in penance.[27] Understanding the ritual as a penitential/reconciliation ritual would be defended in the work of at least one scholar, who writes

That the imposition of hands for the conferring of the Spirit upon heretics was considered as a reconciliation rite is made especially clear by the fact that it involved irregularity for the reception of holy orders and degradation of clerics to the lay state.[28]

Another scholar interprets this "penitential language" as being connected with the desired effect of the ritual: the greatest gift of the Holy Spirit *(donum maximum Spiritus Sancti).*[29]

A key text is a letter of Innocent I (early fifth century), already mentioned, where we read, "We receive them under the image of penance and the sanctification of the Holy Spirit through the imposition of hands *(sub imagine poenitentiae ac sancti Spiritus sanctificatione per manus impositionem suscipimus)."* The *ac* is the key to understanding the text.[30] While he will admit some connection with the "image" of penance, the connection is not strong, because the conjunction *ac* joins two members of the phrase *(imagine poenitentiae* and *sancti Spiritus sanctificatione).* There is no connection between penitents and heretics.

> There is no equivalence, or resemblance between *imago paenitentiae* and the imposition of hands which would be understood here for reconciliation. . . . This *manus impositio* cannot be other than a ceremony well known by all: the *Spiritus sanctificatio* that accomplishes the reconciliation and is normally identified with the rite of initiation.[31]

The prayer over heretics should not be considered to be of the same genre as the absolution prayer over penitents. "To the sinner, one gives that which is lost: the grace and the possession of the Holy Spirit; to the heretic, one gives that which is not yet there."[32]

An abjuration of heresy is also required of the heretic. In the late Middle Ages this would become the overshadowing image of the ritual. This abjuration is first mentioned in canon 8 from Nicaea (325). It is repeated in canon 7 from the Council of Laodicea (343–381) and mentioned also at the Second Ecumenical Council in 381, canon 7. Gregory the Great[33] writes an abjuration of errors and profession of faith that would be used by William Durandus.[34]

Initiation Aspects

Rebaptism: This position was defended strongly by a number of theologians and bishops in the patristic period beginning with Tertullian.[35] The heretics do not possess the Holy Spirit, therefore they are incapable of administering baptism. Cyprian held that these people were not being *rebaptized* but *baptized* since they were never really baptized to begin with.[36] The Donatists in the fourth century would adopt the practice of rebaptizing converts to their schismatic group from the orthodox (catholic) church. The practice was formally renounced by the African Catholic church at the Council of Carthage (345–348). The letter from Pope Siricius I to the bishops of Spain indicates that rebaptism was practiced by some of the bishops. He formally prohibits this.

Certain categories of heretics, however, would be required to undergo baptism for entrance into the church. The Council of Nicaea, for example, requires rebaptism for Montanists (canon 8). Similar distinctions are made for various groups holding unorthodox doctrine on the Trinity.[37] These are exceptions to the general rule: Baptism with proper doctrine (in the name of the Trinity) and with water is valid.

Repetition of Confirmation: Many scholars will identify the reconciliation of heretics with a conferral (or re-conferral) of the sacrament of confirmation. Leo the Great uses language traditionally associated with the sacrament.[38] Texts from Gaul and Spain point to the reception of heretics with an imposition of hands and an anointing, clearly reminiscent of what would come to be known as the sacrament of confirmation.[39] This seems to have been the custom in the Orient and may have been carried to Gaul and Spain from the Orient.[40]

The sacrament of confirmation, however, was believed to be indelible, essential to initiation and unrepeatable.[41] Gregory the Great summarizes that heretics are received either by the anointing of Christ or by the imposition of the hand or by a mere profession of faith,[42] the three modes that were familiar to him.

The mode of reception and the understanding of the reception ritual and its meaning underwent gradual change in the church's tradition. Preconceived notions of seeing the ritual as confirmation or penance inhibit a genuine understanding of the ritual and its effects. The penitential imagery used is best understood as *the* fundamental Christian attitude needed for living fully the Christian life in the Holy Spirit.[43] Understanding the reconciliation of heretics as linked in some way with Christian initiation will help understand the tradition.

Imposition of Hands: Pope Siricius I indicates that an imposition of hands with the invocation of the sevenfold gift of the Holy Spirit is to be made over the one being received. Innocent I makes the distinction that the heretically baptized (Novatians and Montanists) should be received *by the imposition of hands only.*[44] The imposition of hands is mentioned by many of the writers.[45] The First Council of Arles (314) mentions that for those who have been validly baptized "only the hand should be imposed upon him, in order that he may receive the Holy Spirit." Augustine defends the validity of the sacraments outside the church, even though they are inefficacious because they lack the fullness of the Holy Spirit, which can only be experienced within the unity of the church. Hands are imposed upon the candidate for the gift of the Holy Spirit. In this, the candidate receives the gift of charity, which is given to one with the proper disposition. This imposition of hands is simply a prayer over the person *(oratio super hominem),* which according to St. Augustine is repeatable. Thus received, the person can live the fullness of Christian life in the unity of the Holy Spirit, which reigns in the church.[46]

Conclusion

The essential ritual element for the reconciliation of heretics in the patristic period was the imposition of hands with the invocation of the Holy Spirit. Gallican and Visigothic traditions also shows that an anointing with chrism accompanied the reception.

Chapter 2

The Medieval Liturgical Books

■

In the medieval liturgical books, orations are found for the reception/reconciliation of those baptized outside the church's communion. In the oldest collection of formularies, the *Sacramentarium Veronense,* no formularies are found. The earliest witness of orations for this is from the Old Gelasian Sacramentary *(Gelasianum vetus),* an eighth-century copy of a seventh-century liturgical book used in Rome. It is generally accepted among scholars that it contains material that is much older, some from the sixth century.

The Sacramentaries

Gelasianum vetus

The *Gelasianum vetus* (GeV)[1] contains a series of prayers over Arians, and other heretics returning to the Catholic church, and a group of prayers for those who had been rebaptized on going over to another group.[2] The "blessing over those who are coming back to Catholic unity from the Arians" is a prototype of the prayer that will be copied from book to book and used throughout the Middle Ages. It includes the element of imposition of the seven-fold gifts of the Holy Spirit that we saw indicated at least from the time of Pope Siricius I (384).

> Lord God almighty, Father of our Lord Jesus Christ who deigned to pluck away [your servants] from the error and deceit (falsehood) of the Arian heresy and lead them towards your catholic church; Pour out on them, O Lord, the Holy Spirit, the Paraclete of wisdom and understanding, the spirit of counsel and fortitude, the spirit of knowledge and piety and fill them Lord with the spirit of the fear of God, in the Name of Jesus Christ our Savior God, through whom and with whom is to you honor and glory for the ages of ages. Amen. (GeV, 683)

Given the proximity of Gregory's pontificate (590–604) to the supposed time period for the composition of the *Gelasianum vetus* (early 600s), one could hypothesize that this oration was used in conjunction with an imposition of hands.[3] Citing the Council of Arles I (314), F. Quinn concludes, "Handlaying with prayer for the Holy Spirit is the rite intended to perfect baptism or admit heretics to the church."[4]

The oration is addressed to the Father in relation to Christ. In this address, and in the entire prayer, there may be some anti-Arian concerns.[5] The conclusion of the prayer includes an anti-Arian refutation, praying "in the Name of Jesus Christ our Savior God, through whom and with whom is to you honor and glory for the ages of ages."[6]

Following the address, the amplification shows the purpose of the prayer: "who deigned to pluck away [your servants] from the error and deceit of the Arian heresy and lead them toward your catholic church." The prayer emphasizes that it is the work of God that brings the person or persons from the falsehood and error of Arianism to the Catholic church. The language used is a literary convention that implies the reception of a free gift from God.[7] The title of the oration, too, contains an interesting use of terminology: "Catholic unity" means "being led to the Catholic church" *(ad ecclesiam tuam catholicam).*

The second half of the prayer is the prayer for the seven-fold gifts of the spirit *(oratio septiformis donorum).* The oration asks God to send the Holy Spirit, the paraclete *(spiritum paraclytum sanctum)* to the servants, enumerating the seven gifts of the Spirit: *sapientia, intellectus, consilium, fortitudo, scientia, pietas* and *timor dei.* This prayer is of some antiquity; allusion is made to it by Ambrose *(De Sacramentis* III, II.8) and Siricius I. In fact, Pope Siricius I speaks about the reconciliation of Arians "by the invocation of the seven-fold gifts of the spirit with the imposition of hands" *(per invocationem solam septiformis Spiritus, episcopalis manus impositione).*[8] This could be a sign that the prayer (in some form) was known and used as early as the fourth century.[9]

The other oration over people coming from other heresies (GeV, 684) is very similar to the first prayer in structure, language and style. The prayers over those who had been rebaptized *(Reconciliatio rebaptizatis ab heredicis)* take on a different form, language and tone. These prayers have a more penitential cast to them. While these orations are for *lapsi,* or "true apostates"—those who had once been baptized Catholic and were subsequently rebaptized in a heretical sect (and this is not the principal focus of the study)—it is interesting to note a few important details in these orations. There are no indications of the ritual that accompany these prayers. The language of the prayer is penitential in tone, as opposed to language in GeV, 683, which seems to be more initiatory with its pneumatic emphasis.[10]

The language used indicates that this prayer was used for someone who was once part of the church *(ad veram matrem aeclesiam catholicam . . . redeunt).*[11] The oration indicates that the sacrament of baptism is made holy by God; repeating baptism inflicts injury on the faith and harms the other sacraments *(sed iniuria fidei sacramentis manentibus inrogatur)*.[12] The apostate's offense is having insulted that which was permanent in itself, namely baptism. It seems that this oration was intended for those who had been rebaptized by Arians, and that some sort of abjuration may have been made in conjunction with the reconciliation. As in the other prayers, though with a different expression, the return of the apostate to the church is seen as the gracious, free gift of God. In this prayer, the entire community begs of God the gift of reconciliation for the apostate, using the first person plural verb forms *(Unde quaesumus . . . remittatur impietas; probamur; audemus; confidimus; ignoramus; amittimus)*. The prayer concludes with the hope that the effect of penance will not be forgotten and the contrition (or repentance) granted will continue.

The other two prayers in this group are intended for children who were rebaptized in heretical sects. Again in one of the prayers the Arian heresy is mentioned *(nequicia Arrianae perfidiae)*. Both of the orations address God as creator and redeemer of the human race. The prayers petition that the young person not be considered guilty of that which he or she could not understand. The prayers petition that the person again be considered a member of the church, and one of the prayers has as a purpose of the request: that the person be restored to the eucharist *(ut ad altaribus sacris recepta . . . reddatur)*.

In summary, there are a number of tentative conclusions to be drawn from this brief study of the orations from the *Gelasianum vetus*. The prayer over Arians and the prayer over those from other heresies, with the petition for the gifts of the Spirit, links the reconciliation of heretics with Christian initiation and the necessity of the invocation of the Holy Spirit. This follows the pattern of a number of the patristic texts discussed in chapter 1 (i.e., the ritual includes some kind of invocation of the Holy Spirit for admittance to the eucharist and the church). The three orations over the rebaptized have more of a penitential tone. These orations emphasize that it is the devil that causes the straying and its effects. Because of the lack of exact ritual directions, it is impossible to conclude with certainty what kind of ritual action accompanied the orations. However, with the supporting evidence of patristic texts, it can be hypothesized that the prayers were used in conjunction with an imposition of hands.

Two sacramentaries from the Mozarabic tradition preserve well-developed rituals for the reconciliation of heretics. The *Liber Ordinum,* parts of which were in use from the fifth century, preserves a long ritual for the reconciliation of Arians. [13] It includes a detailed renunciation of the Arian heresy, along with a three-fold profession of faith (adapted for the Arian heretic), and an imposition of hands, chrismation and prayer for the Holy Spirit. The chrismation is done with a special formula.[14] After the chrismation, the imposition of the hand is clearly noted, while the "confirmation prayer" is prayed.[15] The classic prayer for the seven-fold gift is part of this prayer.

A brief analysis of the oration offers several interesting insights. The address is very simple, *Deus,* followed by an amplification that makes reference to the unity of believers. Next is a list of the errors of the Arians: They were mixed up in a patricidal sect and wished to divide the Father from the Son; and they negated the incarnation and separated the Holy Spirit from God. Some of the attributes of orthodox faith follow: veneration of the indivisible Trinity; belief in God, creator of all things, and the remission of sins; and belief in the resurrection of the flesh.

The petition of the prayer is most interesting. In it reference is made to the servant, already converted to God, at long last returning to the truth. The desire is expressed that the one returning will remain in firm communion with the church. This is a church in which there is no heresy, perversity, division or impiety, but only true and lasting peace. It is a church founded by divine grace, strengthened by the doctrine of the apostles and held together by holy faith. Allusion is made to the eucharist that will soon be offered.[16]

The different lists of attributes give a strong indication of the didactic character of the prayer.[17] It is definitely a reconciliation *ordo* with clear elements linking the ritual to Christian initiation: asking of the name (twice); the creed and the chrismation followed by the prayer for the seven-fold gift within the confirmation prayer, which is a variant of the prayer found in the baptismal rite.[18] This sacramentary also includes prayers over those baptized in any other unspecified heresy as well as a special prayer for the reconciliation of Donatists.

Sacramentary of Ripoll

The Sacramentary of Ripoll *(Sacramentarium Rivipullense)*[19] is another witness of the Mozarabic tradition from the eleventh century. This sacramentary merits special mention because it is used later in the tradition in the composition of the *ordo* for the reconciliation of heretics in a thirteenth-century pontifical. A ritual for the reconciliation of those converting from the apostates, judaism, heresies or paganism[20] is placed between a series of Mass formularies for the communion of the saints and a votive Mass for the Holy Trinity. The *ordo* contains a blessing with water, three-fold insufflation (breathing) by the bishop on the convert, an exorcism, an entrance into the church, prostration by the convert while three psalms are prayed, *Kyrie,* Lord's Prayer, *Salvum fac,* an oration,[21] three-fold renunciation of Satan, consignation with chrismation, imposition of hands and penance given, and communion.

The Pontificals

The medieval pontificals are another category of liturgical books that were used for organizing the bishop's liturgy. It included the special instructions accompanying prayers or the indication of orations to be used for the special liturgies conducted by the bishop.

Romano-Germanic Pontifical

The tenth-century Romano-Germanic Pontifical includes the same series of prayers that we know already from the *Gelasianum vetus*.[22] The titles have been changed slightly to indicate that some of the prayers are used with an imposition of hands. No indication is given of any anointing.

Pontifical of William Durandus

The later pontificals of the twelfth and thirteenth century have none of these orations, nor do they have an *ordo* for the reconciliation of heretics. The late-thirteenth-century compilation of William Durandus, known as the *Pontifical of William Durandus* (PGD), includes a fully developed *ordo* for the reconciliation of heretics, schismatics and apostates.[23] The *ordo* that he created takes elements from the baptismal ritual used at that time as well as some elements from the Mozarabic *Sacramentarium Rivipullense*. In the pontifical, this ritual is found among 25 new creations of Durandus.[24] The fact that this *ordo* was a new construction by Durandus would seem to indicate that there was a need for such a ritual for the reception of the subjects in question, and that the ritual was actually used.[25]

The ritual begins with questions about the faith at the doors of the church. After this an exorcism is prayed. The text of this prayer does not have any parallels in the tradition of the Roman sacramentaries. The oration is taken from the *Sacramentarium Rivipullense*.[26] It seems that

Durandus may have taken some inspiration from this sacramentary, even though this is the only text he copies from this source.[27] The *ordo* also includes clear indication for a chrismation and consignation, but no indication of an imposition of hands. Durandus chose a different ritual solution. The person is signed with the cross and invited to enter the church. These actions are all reminiscent of the medieval baptismal ritual. The person is invited into the church of God,[28] from which he wandered. The prayer (with use of the imperative) tells the person to "Abhor idols and reject all depravity or superstition of heresy, apostasy or Judaism." The person is commanded to worship the living God.[29] Recalling several scriptural images, the oration recalls that God is always the one who searches out the lost, and rejoices at the conversion of all.

A prayer taken from the *Gelasianum vetus* follows. The petition of the prayer asks that whatever deception was caused by the devil be taken away and the person be returned to the eucharist. The profession of faith follows with the three-part questions on the creed, reminiscent of the questions in the baptismal ritual.[30] Satan was considered the father of all heresies, hence Durandus considered an explicit, ritual renunciation of him and his influence to be important in this context.[31] The renunciation of Satan is done in a question format. The questions are very similar to those found in the *Sacramentarium Rivipullense*.[32] The last question, Do you wish to be and live in union with the holy Catholic church? seems to be inspired by the initiation ritual.[33]

The rubrics indicate that an imposition of the hand is to accompany the next oration. Durandus made a clear choice to follow a certain strand of the tradition as he knew it. This tradition had many witnesses, from conciliar teaching, local bishops and Roman pontiffs.[34] The oration given has many parallels in the tradition.[35] Given the earlier choices of Durandus, it is likely that he took this prayer from an eighth-century sacramentary: The oration does not use *mater* (mother) as an attribute of the church (which Durandus added to one of the orations above). The closing phrase with the passive, *signetur* (be signed), would further indicate an eighth-century Frankish-Gelasian source.[36] There is no indication here or in any other place in the *ordo* of Durandus for an anointing with chrism, which is explicitly mentioned with a formula in the *Sacramentarium Rivipullense*.[37] Durandus deliberately chose to omit the anointing, preferring not to identify the reconciling of heretics with the sacrament of confirmation while affirming the value of the traditional imposition of hands for the invocation of the Holy Spirit.[38]

Two long abjurations follow, one for schismatics and one for heretics. The abjuration of schism is meant to be a public profession of fidelity to the church and a renunciation of errors. The text comes from a letter of Gregory the Great, in the seventh century.[39] In Gregory's time, this text was used for people coming to the church who had instituted a schism; in fact, the text seems to have been drafted for the reconciliation of a schismatic bishop. From the tenth century on, the abjuration of heresy gradually grew in importance in the ritual to overshadow what had been the central gestures, the imposition of hands and/or the anointing with chrism, accompanied by prayer.[40] The abjuration found here is included in the Decree of Gratian (a twelfth-century collection of canon law texts).[41] This abjuration, originally used for the heretic Berengar in the eleventh century,[42] is for the founders or spreaders of heresy.[43] The heretics were also required to make a public profession of faith and abjuration of their errors, as well as an oath to the holy Roman pontiff and the church. The abjuration is in the tradition from at least the time of Tertullian.[44]

Summation

Penitential Aspects

In the medieval liturgical books, the orations that indicate a penitential tone or have images of penance are associated with those who were "true apostates" (who are somewhat outside the scope of this study). Even those who were rebaptized under force or fear are reconciled with prayers using penitential imagery.[45] The ritual gesture used (in the Mozarabic tradition) is the imposition of hands. Penitential imagery (in orations) and gestures in the reconciliation of those originally heretically baptized are not part of the medieval tradition.[46]

Initiation Aspects

Rebaptism: For the reconciliation of heretics, the tradition shows a strong current beginning with Tertullian and continued by Cyprian, of rebaptism (or rather "baptism" since the persons were never really baptized to begin with). In the medieval liturgical books there are no indications that rebaptism was practiced.

Repetition of Confirmation: The repeating of "confirmation" is an area of more difficulty. Certainly there are elements in the orations and tradition that resemble what could be identified with the sacrament of confirmation. Already, in the *Gelasianum vetus* (GeV, 683, 684), pneumatic elements are present in the oration with the presence of the prayer for the seven-fold gift of the Holy Spirit. This portion of the prayer occurs in the majority of the orations and/or rituals for the reconciliation of the heretically baptized. This builds on a tradition long witnessed in ancient patristic texts. The Holy Spirit had to be conferred on the person to "complete" or "perfect" the (somehow) deficient baptism received from the heretical minister.

It was shown that some of the eighth-century sacramentaries augmented this part of the prayer, copied from the *Gelasianum vetus,* with words indicating a consignation (signing). This consignation, however, need not be identified with an anointing with chrism. Durandus includes a consignation in the prayer for the gifts without an anointing.[47]

The *ordo* for the reconciliation of Arians in the *Liber ordinum* (Mozarabic) includes an anointing with chrism for the reconciliation of heretics.[48] Several Gallican councils also witness to a reconciliation of heretics with an anointing, but no evidence of an anointing is found in the Gallican sources (i.e., the Gelasian family of sacramentaries). Perhaps this tradition did not survive in any of the sacramentaries that are still preserved. Pope Gregory II (715–731) wrote to Boniface, bishop of Mainz, that confirmation is not to be repeated.

Imposition of Hands: The indications that the imposition of hands was the ritual action *par excellence* for the reconciliation of the heretically baptized is strong. While no indications are found in the medieval sacramentaries, a witness almost contemporary with the *Gelasianum vetus* indicates that in the West, Arians were received by the imposition of hands.[49] The tenth-century Romano-Germanic Pontifical takes the prayers from the medieval sacramentaries, augmenting the title to include an imposition of hands.[50] It would seem logical that with the change of title the redactors of this pontifical would have made mention of an anointing if one were to be included.

By the time of Durandus, an imposition of hands with the prayer for the sending of the Holy Spirit was considered the proper ritual action for receiving heretics, schismatics and apostates into the church. With the order for reconciliation created by him, modeled in part on the baptismal ritual (e.g., with the ritual beginning at the doors of the church and inclusion of an exorcism), Durandus makes a clear choice for the imposition of hands. The ritual also includes two abjurations of error, one for schismatics and one for heretics. This is not to be understood as a repetition of confirmation. The *ordo* follows the tradition that the Holy Spirit needs to be conferred on those baptized outside the church. To use the words of Saint-Palais d'Aussac, this is less than a confirmation and more than a reconciliation (of penitents).

Conclusion

The Roman tradition of accepting the validity of baptism outside the church found liturgical expression in the medieval liturgical books. This position, first articulated by Stephen I (254–257), came up against opposition, yet is gradually accepted as the Roman church's position. A prayer for the seven-fold gifts is a universal part of the known Western tradition. The consolidation of the medieval books in the creative redaction work of William Durandus leaves the church with an *ordo* for reconciliation reminiscent of the baptismal ritual, following initiation concepts (i.e., exorcisms, consignations, profession of faith and invocation of the Holy Spirit). The abjuration of heresy (or schism) became very important, almost overshadowing the primary gesture, the imposition of hands. With the next chapter, our study will investigate the church's ritual practice from the Post-Tridentine period to the eve of Vatican II.

Chapter 3

The Modern History

■

The validity of a baptism performed outside the Catholic church was strongly held in the Western tradition at least from the time of Pope Stephen I (d. 254). This tradition is reinforced with development in the Modern period.[1]

Sixteenth-Century Councils

The Council of Trent (1545–1563), in Session VII (1547), dealt with the question of the sacraments in general, and each one in particular. The Council reiterated the traditional teaching about the validity of baptism outside the church. Canon 9, on the sacraments in general, summarizes the doctrine about the permanent "character" that is imprinted on the soul in baptism, confirmation and orders, and the nonrepeatability of these sacraments.[2] Canons 4 and 11 uphold the validity of baptism performed outside the church in the name of the Trinity, and the impossibility of repeating baptism even for those who have denied the faith.

A synod of bishops meeting in Rouen in 1581 discussed the nature of the reception into the church of those baptized by the Calvinists. The bishops evidently knew of the order for the reconciliation of apostates, schismatics or heretics from the *Pontifical of William Durandus*.[3] They discussed the question of whether such a ritual was to be applied to baptized protestants. The bishops noted, in effect, that baptism in the Calvinist tradition did not have all the ceremonies of Catholic baptism.[4]

A most interesting discussion is reported in the proceedings of the Council. The bishops generally held one of three positions. One group refuted the practice of supplying the ceremonies absent in the Calvinist baptism. They understood the tradition to call only for the imposition of hands on the person, an action that they understood as confirmation. For this group the hand-laying of reconciliation and the sacrament of confirmation were the same thing. Another group held for the supplying of ceremonies omitted in the Calvinist baptism, as had been done in the past for those who had not received chrismation in a non-Catholic baptism. The missing ceremonies were supplied upon their entrance into the church. For this group, this imposition of hands was absolution and reconciliation, not a confirmation. A third group tried to find a middle ground. They didn't want to apply the ceremonies that would be too humiliating to the Calvinists, such as the exorcisms.[5]

The Council sought counsel from the Holy See about its discussion. Gregory XIII (1572–1585) replied to the bishops that the ceremonies lacking should be supplied, preceded (in the case of adults) with an abjuration of heresy and a reconciliation.[6] He did not say anything about the historical question under discussion at the Council of Rouen: What is the meaning of the imposition of hands in the reconciliation of heretics?[7] The

Pontificale Romanum issued following the Council of Trent would include an order for reconciliation.

Sixteenth-Century Liturgical Practice

Pontificale Romanum 1595

The *Pontificale Romanum* was not published until some 30 years after the end of the Council of Trent.[8] This work was a direct descendant of the *Pontifical of William Durandus,* drawn up in the late-thirteenth century. Part III of the *Pontificale Romanum* contains an order for the reconciliation of apostates, schismatics or heretics. A ceremony is included for the expulsion of public penitents from the church on Ash Wednesday. The *ordo* includes the penitential psalms and prayers for conversion. Also found in this liturgical book is a liturgy for the reconciliation of penitents on Holy Thursday.[9] This is the liturgy of readmittance to the eucharist for grave sinners (not heretics and schismatics) who entered into public penance on Ash Wednesday.[10] However beautiful these liturgies are, the fact is that their inclusion was gratuitous. The three liturgies mentioned here were included in the *Pontificale* by Clement VIII for historical purposes rather than pastoral reasons.[11] It should also be noted that this edition of the *Pontificale* has no ritual for baptism.[12]

The ritual for the reconciliation of apostates, schismatics or heretics is almost the same as the *ordo* created by William Durandus, presented in the previous chapter, but a few changes were made:

- The *ordo* is designed exclusively for the bishop.[13]

- Twelve questions are included in the interrogation of faith.[14]

- The one being reconciled is led by the hand of the bishop into the church.[15]

- It is specified that the bishop imposes the *right* hand on the person's head.[16]

- The final clause of the pneumatic prayer is changed from "Fill (him) with the spirit of the fear of the Lord" *(adimple eum spiritu timoris domini)* to "Fill (him) with the light of your splendor" *(adimple eum lumine splendoris tui)*.[17]

- The abjuration of errors for schismatics and heretics is slightly modified.[18]

These changes are mostly minor, and in substance the ritual is that created by Durandus in the thirteenth century.

Rituale Romanum 1614

The *Rituale Romanum* published in 1614 (RR 1614) has often been regarded as a liturgical creation of the Tridentine reform. Part II of this ritual contains the orders for baptism. Chapter III of Part II contains the *praenotanda* for adult baptism; paragraphs 11 and 12 are relevant for our purposes.

> 11. In every case where, after due investigation, a reasonable doubt remains as to whether the person has been baptized really or validly, baptism should be administered again conditionally.

> 12. Prospective converts to the Catholic church from heresy, in whose baptism either the necessary form or the matter was not used, should be baptized absolutely. But first they must be duly instructed in the Catholic faith. In a case, however, where in baptism by heretics the necessary form and matter were used, only the rest of the ceremonies should be added, unless the Ordinary decides otherwise for a good reason.[19]

These paragraphs are quite simple and merely indicate the cases in which absolute or conditional baptism should be given, and the cases in which a person is received into the church by means of a renunciation of heresy and the supplying of ceremonies that were not a part of their previous (heretical) baptism.[20] These directions fall clearly in line with the long tradition of the church.

Chapter IV of the *Rituale* contains the complete *ordo* for an adult baptism. For this study it is enough to note the things that are inserted specifically for those who wished to come to the Catholic church from other religious traditions. The renunciation of false worship for each kind of person:

> *If the candidate is a convert from paganism, the priest adds:* Abhor idols and reject their images.
>
> *If from Judaism:* Abhor Jewish infidelity, renounce the false belief of the Hebrews.
>
> *If from Mohammedanism:* Abhor Islam's infidelity, renounce this evil and faithless sect.
>
> If the candidate belonged to a Protestant sect, and the validity of previous baptism is in question, he says: Abhor the evil of heresy, renounce the infamous sect of N. (mentioning the name of the sect.)
>
> *The priest continues:* Worship God, the Father almighty, and Jesus Christ, His Sole-Begotten Son, our Lord, Who shall come to judge the living and the dead and the world by fire. Amen.[21]

and the conditional baptism directions and formula:

> *But if there should be a reasonable doubt as to whether the candidate has been validly baptized before, the priest says:* N., If thou are not baptized, I baptize thee in the name of the Father, and of the Son and of the Holy Spirit.[22]

Those coming from Jewish or Islamic traditions and the pagans were, obviously, never baptized; thus, the celebration of the order for the baptism of adults would be celebrated in its entirety. They would be baptized absolutely with the appropriate renunciation of false worship pronounced.

If there was a doubt regarding the validity of the baptism of a person coming from a protestant group, conditional baptism was conferred according to the above formula. The appropriate renunciation of false worship against the particular protestant sect is mentioned, and the appropriate absolution from excommunication was given by the priest. A commentator on the *Rituale Romanum* notes that two processes actually take place.

> The priest who receives him takes away the impediment of excommunication, thereby restoring him to the rights given, all unconsciously, by the heretical minister who baptized him . . . [and celebrates] the ceremonies omitted in the heretical baptism. . . . In the case of a person doubtfully baptized, no one can say which of these two processes really takes place. The priest baptizes conditionally as a precaution for the one case, and hears his confession for the other. Both sacraments, baptism and penance, are administered conditionally, and the one or the other, as the case requires, is certainly valid.[23]

At the end of the baptismal ritual is a notation for when a bishop is present at the ceremony:

> If a bishop is present who can lawfully do so, he should forthwith confer the sacrament of confirmation on the newly baptized.

> Then if the hour be suitable, Mass is celebrated, at which the neophytes assist and devoutly receive the Holy Eucharist.[24]

From this inclusion, one understands that the sacrament of confirmation was to be administered immediately to the newly baptized adult only if a bishop were present.

Chapter VI contains the *ordo* for supplying ceremonies omitted in baptism. This ritual is practically identical to the full order of adult baptism, except for two changes: The introductory verse and psalms are done if there is time, and the actual baptism is omitted. This ritual recognizes that the person has been validly baptized.[25] In principle, all that is needed is that he be absolved from the excommunication incurred by being part of a heretical sect. The RR 1614 provides for the supplying of the ceremonies omitted in the heretical baptism.[26] As we will see in the presentation of particular legislation for the Catholic church in the United States, the ordinary often granted a dispensation from the supplying of these ceremonies.[27]

An anomaly in this *ordo* for the supplying of ceremonies is the Command to Renounce False Worship for

Jews, pagans and Moslems. Clearly, these three religions have no practice of baptism that would be considered valid, so it seems strange that these are included in this ritual. An explanation for the inclusion of the entire Renunciation would assume a mere exact copying of the order for adult baptism, dropping only the baptismal formula.

A similar notation about confirmation is given as in the complete order of baptism above. If the newly received needs to be confirmed and a bishop is present, he is immediately to confirm the newly received, and if possible, celebrate the Mass and give communion to the newly received. This is noteworthy because the phrase "if they are to be confirmed" would indicate that some categories of people received into the church need not be confirmed (orthodox Christians). In addition, if necessary, the person should proceed to sacramental confession before being confirmed.[28]

Collectio Rituum

The *Collectio Rituum* is a select collection of various orders from the RR 1614 and other sources prepared for the use of the clergy of a particular region or country. A *Collectio Rituum* was first published in 1954 for use in the United States.[29] A second *Collectio Rituum* was published in 1961, and a later edition was published in 1964. The rubrics of this book correspond to the rubrics of the edition of the *Rituale Romanum* 1614 that had been edited with the addition of elements from the 1917 *Code of Canon Law* and published in Rome in 1952 (RR 1614/1952).[30] The 1954 *Collectio Rituum* included only the rituals for the baptism of one (or several) infant(s), and for the supplying of ceremonies for baptized infants. The *Collectio Rituum* published in 1961 included extensive baptismal orders for the use of the parish priest and the bishop.[31] The *Collectio Rituum* published in 1964 included baptismal rites and a ceremony for the reception of converts.[32]

Let us note the differences between the RR 1614/1952 and the *Collectio Rituum* of 1964. In the order for the baptism of adults in the *Collectio Rituum* 1964, the ritual comprises the same elements as in the RR 1614, except that the renunciation of false worship is dropped. This was abolished by the Sacred Congregation of Rites as a logical consequence of the Holy Week reforms of 1955.[33] (This collection also contains an order for the baptism of adults arranged according to the stages of the catechumenate that was promulgated 16 April 1962.[34])

Chapter III of the *Collectio Rituum* includes the rituals for the sacrament of penance: the common form of absolution and absolution from excommunication outside of sacramental confession. The chapter includes an order titled The Reception of Converts. This rite finds its genesis in a decree issued from the Holy Office in 1859. It is designed for the reception into the Catholic church of the validly baptized. It seems odd to read in the *praenotanda* directions for those needing to be "absolutely baptized," those needing to be "conditionally baptized" and those whose baptism is judged valid, since this order seems to be intended only for those who had received valid baptism. The abjuration of heresy or profession of faith alone is received, followed by the absolution from censures.

After noting that the priest is to vest in violet, the rite then directs that the convert kneel before the priest, touch the Book of Gospels with the right hand and make the profession of faith following the formulas provided (one is shorter and intended for the less educated). This formula is both an abjuration of heresy and a profession of faith. The profession of faith was originally given in the decree of 1859. A new text for the profession of faith was prepared in 1942; it is that text which is used in the order presented here.[35]

Next, the priest is directed to pray Psalms 50 and 129, a litany with the *kyrie eleison, Pater noster* and *Salvum fac,*[36] and the following prayer:

> O God, to whom it belongs always to show mercy and to spare, receive our prayer, that this your servant, bound by the penalty of excommunication, may be pardoned by your mercy. Through Christ . . . [37]

After this, the absolution from heresy follows:

> By apostolic authority, which I exercise in this matter, I absolve you from the bond of excommunication which you have (perhaps) incurred, and I restore you to the holy sacraments of the church, and to the communion and unity with the faithful, in the name of the Father . . . [38]

The priest is directed to assign a light penance, and that is the end of the ceremony.

The ritual is very brief and direct. Except in the introductory notes, there is no equivocation in this ceremony about the validity of baptism: This *ordo* is for those definitely, validly baptized who wish to be received into the Catholic church. In the context of this study, there are a number of points that are striking about this *ordo*.

- The *ordo* is linked to a penitential understanding of the reception of converts, because it is included among the various penitential orders, and a penance is imposed.

- The abjuration of heresy assumed a role of major importance and the traditional imposition of hands has disappeared.

Other Ecclesiastical Documents

In addition to the liturgical/ritual history of the *ordo* for the reception of the validly baptized into the church, other church documents need to be taken into account. The Holy Office issued two instructions concerning the reception of converts (1859 and 1878), and the Provincial and Plenary Councils of Baltimore (1791–1884) issued canons that affected liturgical practice in the United States. The *Code of Canon Law* promulgated in 1917 has several canons on baptism.

Holy Office Instruction of 20 July 1859

An Instruction was prepared in response to a question from the archbishop of Philadelphia as a clarification of the law that required converts to make a profession of faith and to be absolved from the censure of excommunication. It gives the following information:

> In the conversion of heretics, the first inquiry needs to be about the validity of the baptism received in heresy. Therefore, after a diligent examination has been made, if it is found that no baptism was conferred, or that it was conferred invalidly, they are to be baptized absolutely. If, when the investigation is completed, the validity of the baptism is still in doubt, baptism must be given conditionally *(sub-conditione)*. Finally, if it is established that the baptism received was valid, they are to be received only with the abjuration or profession of faith. . . .
>
> 1. If the baptism is conferred absolutely, no abjuration or absolution follows, as all has been washed away in the sacrament of regeneration.
>
> 2. If baptism is repeated conditionally, this is the order:
>
> a. Abjuration or profession of faith
> b. Conditional baptism
> c. Sacramental confession with conditional absolution.
>
> 3. When the baptism is judged to be valid, abjuration or profession of faith alone and the absolution from censures follows.[39]

The abjuration or profession of faith includes the Creed, the major points of Catholic doctrine, a refutation of errors and an acceptance of the primacy of the Roman pontiff. It is also required that the convert accept the teachings of the councils and "detest and abjure every error, heresy and sect opposed to the said Holy Catholic and Apostolic Roman Church."[40] The convert makes this profession of faith while kneeling before a priest in the sanctuary.[41] The Instruction also indicates that the priest is to be vested with a violet stole and holding the gospel book; the convert touches the gospel book with the right hand while reciting the abjuration/ profession of faith.[42] The Councils of Baltimore later extend the prescriptions of this Instruction to every diocese, even though it was issued to the local church of Philadelphia.[43] This abjuration/profession of faith was augmented by a modified text issued in 1942.[44] In this Instruction there is no mention of the imposition of the hand(s) on the person being received.

Holy Office Instruction of 20 November 1878

The Holy Office issued an instruction on the question of rebaptism in 1878[45] under Pope Leo XIII (1878–1903). This decree merely reiterates previous traditional teaching: Baptism, once validly received, is not to be repeated. Careful investigation is to be undertaken to discern if one has been validly baptized. If one is to be baptized conditionally because it is established that they were not validly baptized, this is to be done privately. If one is determined to have been validly baptized, only the abjuration and profession of faith are necessary for reception. Nothing is mentioned about the liturgical ritual for the reception, and there is no mention of the traditional imposition of hands.

Provincial and Plenary Councils of Baltimore

A series of synods and councils (provincial and plenary) was convoked in the United States between 1791 and 1884. These gatherings of priests and bishops were convoked to unify pastoral practice and provide for the future and growth of Catholic life in the young country.

First National Synod: At the First National Synod (1791), convoked by John Carroll, the first bishop in the United States, the clergy were faced with

> many Catholics who were not certain of having been bap-
> tized; others had been baptized privately; others still had been
> baptized by non-Catholic ministers. To relieve them of their
> anxiety, the church law on rebaptizing *sub-conditione* was
> made clear; but priests were warned to make a thorough
> investigation in each case. . . . In the case of adult converts
> who had been validly baptized, it was necessary only to supply
> the ceremonies.[46]

The decrees on the sacrament of baptism indicates the bishops' concern to provide clear, correct teaching on baptism: Baptism is an important sacrament and a special character is imprinted on the soul upon its valid reception. In the earlier meetings of the bishops of the country, priests were encouraged to "act cautiously" in the cases of people validly baptized. While this could be interpreted as an encouragement to presume validity, it seems that in pastoral practice it was taken negatively. Thus, the validity of most non-Catholic baptisms was considered doubtful.

First Plenary Council of Baltimore: At the First Plenary Council of Baltimore in 1852, "the concession of using the shorter form of infant baptism for the baptism of adults was to be asked for in perpetuity."[47] A decree was issued from the Congregation for the Propagation of the Faith, 26 September 1852, granting this concession for five years.[48] "The same petition was renewed in the Council of 1866 without any general extension being granted. The Council of 1884, after repeating the warning to ascertain the status of any previous baptism, instructs priests to receive converts into the church by the Instruction of 1859."[49]

Second Plenary Council of Baltimore: The Second Plenary Council of Baltimore offered a more detailed treatment of the issues surrounding the reception of those validly baptized outside the church. The Council was convoked in 1866 under the leadership of Archbishop Martin John Spalding.[50] The decrees from this Council connected with this study are decrees 240 to 242, which speak about the gravity of baptism and the problem of rebaptism.[51] Since baptism imprints an indelible character on the soul, one who would rashly presume to rebaptize a convert would be guilty of the gravest crime. However, baptism by heretical ministers was very suspect since it was thought that heretics were accustomed to neglect the most essential ceremonies in their administration of baptism. For this reason, many felt it necessary to rebaptize conditionally practically all converts from heresy. This was prohibited "when there was not present the doubt of the validity of baptism."[52] This decree speaks about the character that is imprinted on the soul at baptism and insists that to rebaptize is a grave offense. "If a priest acted on mere general presumptions rather than on the results of an accurate individual examination of the baptism in heresy, he incurred an irregularity for presuming to baptize without sufficient reason."[53]

Decree 241 indicates that in the case of baptism by a midwife, after diligent investigation, one witness would be sufficient to testify to validity.[54] Decree 242 prescribes the use of the Instruction of 1859 for the Catholic Church in the United States.[55]

Third Plenary Council of Baltimore: The Third Plenary Council of Baltimore was convoked in 1884 under the presidency of Archbishop James Gibbons of Baltimore.[56] This council was called "in order that any abuses which may have crept into American Catholic life be eliminated and that uniform standards of discipline be strengthened by common counsel."[57] A careful look at the acts and decrees of the Third Plenary Council shows that "its legislation is a carefully planned codification of all the laws enacted since the Synod of 1791."[58]

The decrees on the sacraments deal only with the reception of converts and marriage, so we can assume that there were problems with these matters that resulted in the need for more elaboration from the bishops as custodians of the sacraments. The decrees on baptism recall again the character granted the soul at baptism plus a warning to investigate diligently the status of any previous baptism. Priests are again instructed to follow the *ordo* given in the Instruction of 1859 for the reception of converts into the church.

> 122. That due veneration for baptism be preserved, and that all appearances of its illegitimate repetition be removed, the church has prescribed that when one is converted to the faith from error, there must always be a diligent inquiry as to whether he has been baptized before, and whether the baptism received in heresy was valid. A mere general investigation of the custom or practice of certain sects, from which can be had a presumption as to whether or not the baptism was conferred, or as to its validity or nullity, is not sufficient; but, as far as it shall be possible, there must be an inquiry into the baptism of the individual converts, so that the certitude or probability that they were or were not validly baptized may be obtained. When the investigation has been completed, the convert must be received according to the manner described in the Instruction of the Holy Office of the year 1859, which is to be seen in the Appendix of the II Plenary Council of Baltimore and in most ritual books.[59]

Nothing new is added to the previous teaching on this topic.

Code of Canon Law 1917

The *Code of Canon Law* promulgated by Pope Benedict XV in 1917[60] has several canons that treat baptism, the rights and obligations of the baptized and the proper subjects of baptism. A brief look at the pertinent canons will bring us up-to-date with church law to the eve of the Second Vatican Council.

The first two canons that are pertinent for our study serve the general purpose of defining who is and who is not subject to the laws of the church. In the mind of the church, all who are baptized are subject to the laws of the church.

Canon 12 deals with those who are subject to the law of the church:

> Unbaptized persons nor baptized persons who do not have sufficient use of reason and, unless the law expressly rules otherwise, those who, although they have attained the use of reason, have not yet completed their seventh year, are not bound by purely ecclesiastical laws.[61]

Canon 87, written with the influence of canon 7[62] on baptism from the Council of Trent, states:

> A person, in virtue of his baptism, is made a person in the church of Christ with all the rights and obligations of a Christian, unless, with regard to rights, there exists an obstacle which impedes the bond of ecclesiastical union, or a censure imposed by the church.[63]

In these two canons we find that the church has as subjects all who have been baptized. "Irrespective of the minister of baptism," one becomes a member of the church by valid water baptism. "Heretics, schismatics, apostates, and excommunicated persons are, therefore, bound by these laws . . . [because there is imprinted on the soul] . . . an indelible character." However, to benefit from being part of the church of Christ, the person must be

> in communion with the church and free of censure. Communion with the church is lost by the nature of *(ex ipsa natura rei)* apostasy, heresy and schism. *Apostasy* is complete defection from the faith. *Heresy* is a partial defection from the faith resulting from an error of the intellect. *Schism* consists in an error of the will opposed to the social unity of the Catholic church as centered in the authority of the Roman Pontiff. . . .
>
> The canonical juridic capacity of apostates, heretics, schismatics, and the censured remains at least radically intact, but it is incomplete or defective as opposed to the complete and full

> juridic personality of those among the baptized who are not
> affected by these impediments or censures.[64]

In summary, by baptism with water in the name of the
Trinity, people become a part of the church of Christ.

Canon 732, recalling the teaching of the Council of
Trent[65] on the nonrepeatability of the sacraments of
baptism, confirmation and holy orders, states that only if
a prudent doubt exists may any of these sacraments be
conferred again conditionally.

> §1. The sacraments of baptism, confirmation, and holy orders,
> which imprint a character on the soul, cannot be conferred a
> second time.

> §2. But if there should exist a prudent doubt whether they
> were in fact conferred or whether they were validly con-
> ferred, they shall be conferred again conditionally.[66]

It is the "indelible character imprinted on the soul"
that is a "sign of the supernatural union of the baptized
person with Christ." Such "character" constitutes the
baptized person a juridical person in the church "with
all the rights and obligations of a Christian." On this
basis, all the baptized are considered members of the one
church of Christ.[67]

Canon 759 indicates the only instances that are per-
missible for the celebration of a private baptism. The
supplying of ceremonies for those baptized privately was
seen as very important for the complete celebration of
the sacrament.

> Canon 759 §1. It is lawful to confer baptism privately in dan-
> ger of death; and if it is conferred by a minister who is nei-
> ther a priest nor a deacon, only that shall be done which is
> necessary for the validity of the baptism; if by a priest or a
> deacon, the ceremonies that follow baptism shall also be
> observed, if time allows.

> §2. Outside the danger of death the local ordinary cannot
> permit private baptism, except in the case of heretics who are
> conditionally baptized as adults.

> §3. The ceremonies, however, which for any reason were
> omitted in the conferring of baptism, shall be supplied as soon

as possible in church, except in the case just noted in the second paragraph.[68]

If the local ordinary grants permission for the private conditional baptism of adult converts without requiring the use of any ceremonies, it is sufficient to pronounce merely the formula of conditional baptism. "The Second and Third Plenary Council of Baltimore both warn against rebaptism of converts and demand specific investigation of the validity of a previous baptism received in heresy."[69] Attitudes were changing toward some protestant groups, and in 1949 the Holy Office issued a directive to presume the proper intention of a number of protestant sects.[70]

Summation

In the course of this chapter, we have studied in detail the liturgical practice in the period from Trent to the eve of Vatican II and the legislative texts of the church that touch this issue. In the course of this investigation, the following points were reiterated from tradition studied in the previous chapters or further developed in this time period:

- Baptism cannot be repeated.

- For a person validly baptized, only the missing ceremonies are supplied unless the ordinary grants a dispensation.

- Baptism imprints an indelible character on the soul, signifying union with Christ and therefore cannot be repeated.

- Baptism is properly conferred with water and the invocation of the Triune God with the minister having the intention of the church. Thus, baptism given by heretics with the proper matter and form is valid.

- For the reception of a convert, a diligent investigation was demanded to find out the nature of the previous baptism.

- Converts whose baptism was judged valid made a profession of faith and/or abjuration of heresy.

- Those doubtfully baptized made the profession of faith/abjuration, received conditional baptism and made a confession with conditional absolution. For a person to be baptized *sub conditione,* there needed to be a reasonable doubt about the validity of the person's baptism.

- Those never baptized were baptized absolutely with all the ceremonies (unless a dispensation from these was granted) and also made an abjuration of heresy.

- The Councils of Baltimore sought a dispensation from supplying the ceremonies in the United States and for making this process as simple as possible.

- The Holy Office issued an Instruction in 1859 for the reception of converts. This Instruction was made normative for the Catholic church in the United States by the Second Plenary Council of Baltimore. The profession of faith for this was augmented in 1942.

- The 1917 *Code of Canon Law* compiles the previous teaching from the canons of the Council of Trent, the *Rituale Romanum* and later legislation. No new ground is covered in this legislation.

- In 1949, the Holy Office issued a decree accepting as valid the baptism of various protestant sects.

- The imposition of hands as the traditional gesture for the reconciliation of heretics all but disappeared from the *ordo* actually in use.[71]

Conclusion

This summary of the data discovered in the post-Tridentine period will serve as background for the next chapter. It is from the experience of bishops and theologians who were formed in the above tradition that a new attitude toward the reception of converts would develop and grow. We take the above experience into account as we enter into the study of the Conciliar period.

Vatican II and Reform

■

This chapter will follow the development of the *ordo* for the reception of the validly baptized into full communion from the initial days of preparation for the Second Vatican Council to the promulgation of The First Ecumenical Directory in 1967. This document had a direct influence on the development of the *ordo* by the body charged with carrying out the mandates of the Council's liturgy constitution, *Consilium ad exsequendam constitutionem de sacra liturgia (Consilium)*.

Sacrosanctum Concilium

Early in the summer of 1959, following Pope John XXIII's announcement of a gathering of all the bishops of the world in an ecumenical council, a request was sent to all the bishops for their suggestions for topics of discussion at the council. Any "counsels and desires which   **45** they wished to discuss at the future council" would be accepted for consideration.[1] Their replies fill 12 volumes and were carefully collected, recorded and categorized.[2] The collected suggestions on the sacraments fill 186 pages, of which 16 pages are on the sacrament of baptism.

Preparation for the Council

The bishops' suggestions about baptism treat issues ranging from questions from godparents and the baptism of the children of lapsed Catholics to the call for the restoration of the catechumenate.[3] Several bishops asked for clarification of the validity of baptism conferred by protestant churches, an important issue for bishops from countries with a variety of Christian denominations.[4] In some places there were questions about what constituted valid baptism. The baptism performed by a protestant minister may be considered valid in the case of a mixed-religion marriage,[5] and invalid or doubtfully valid if a person were making a profession of faith to join the Catholic church.[6] This was an especially important question for the Catholic church in the United States.

Several suggestions touch the topic of receiving baptized Christians into communion with the Catholic church. Two bishops from Holland called for a more positive approach with people coming from protestant sects. Cardinal Alfrink spoke of a profession of faith before their baptism,[7] revealing that in practice many (if not most) protestants were conditionally baptized on their entry into the Catholic church. Bishop McNamara, an auxiliary bishop from Washington, D.C., suggested that in their continuing formation in the Catholic church these persons have some preparation for confirmation.[8] Archbishop Binz from Dubuque suggested that the restored catechumenate might also serve those converting to the church.[9] Many bishops asked that the baptismal rites be shortened. The baptismal ritual in the

Rituale Romanum of 1614 (RR 1614) was quite long and contained a number of exorcisms and rites. This call for the shortening of existing rites was without doubt also in the minds of those who asked for the development of new rites. No comments were made about the reception of the baptized into full communion.

The commission that made the preparations for the Council in the area of liturgy, *Pontificia Commissio de Sacra Liturgia Praeparatoria Concilii Vaticani II,*[10] met for the first time in the Autumn of 1960, and work began immediately to draft a document on the liturgy. After the first meeting, a subcommission went to work on the drafting of the chapter on the sacraments and sacramentals. In the spring of 1961 the draft was discussed, and after this meeting the secretariat staff pulled the entire work together. It was then sent out for comment, and a third meeting was called in January 1962. The document on the sacred liturgy was discussed, put in final form and presented to the president of the commission for his final approval. On 1 February 1962, Cardinal Cicognani signed the document and passed it on to the Central Commission of the Ecumenical Council. After Cicognani's death (literally a few days after finishing this massive work), Cardinal Arcadio Larraona became the new prefect of the Congregation of Rites and thus presented the draft titled *On the Sacred Liturgy (De sacra liturgia)* to the secretariat of the Council.[11]

When *De sacra liturgia* was presented to the Central Commission, the ritual for receiving a baptized person was placed in paragraph 54 with the ritual for supplying ceremonies for infants baptized in emergency without ceremonies.[12]

> In the place of the order for the supplying of ceremonies in infant baptism, a new rite is to be drawn up for receiving the infant in the parish church which would be a brief rite for the already baptized. In the same way, a new rite was to be

drawn up for the validly baptized newly converted (to the Catholic faith).[13]

One needs to look to the RR 1614 to understand why these two rituals were thought of in the same paragraph. It offers an order for supplying the ceremonies omitted in the baptism of adults similar to the one for infants. For the theologians preparing the draft, it was natural to think of these two rituals together; in the tradition of the church, the supplying of ceremonies was seen as necessary to complete baptism whether in an emergency in the case of infants, or baptism by a protestant minister as in the case of adults coming to communion with the Catholic church.[14]

At the fifth meeting of the Central Commission for the Ecumenical Council, held from 26 March to 3 April 1962, *De sacra liturgia* was presented and discussed. A series of observations was offered by the cardinals on the Central Commission. Bugnini calls this Central Commission a sort of "mini council" that discussed and amended the document before sending it to the fathers of the Council.

Some of the cardinals were concerned about the restoration of the catechumenate. Cardinal Gilroy expressed concern that the catechumenate should be restored only in the mission lands. (Another discussion was the issue of confirmation and the possibility of it being conferred by a priest which, at that time, was permitted only by rare delegation.)[15] Cardinal Alfrink offered the observation that the establishment or nonestablishment of the catechumenate would be left up to the local ordinary or episcopal conference because the needs of the various regions are different. For him and the people of his flock, he notes,

> [M]any adults who are coming to baptism are already Christians because they have been baptized in the protestant religion, even though doubtfully, so that they are rebaptized *sub conditione*. For these, the catechumenate, as it is understood,

is not very fitting. Perhaps for these, it would be better for a shortened rite of adult baptism be drawn up as that mentioned in [an earlier paragraph].

I doubt the utility of the practice, . . . that a newly baptized adult should be given confirmation immediately after baptism by the baptizing priest.

Both theologically and historically, weighty arguments can be brought forward in favor of the administration of confirmation together with baptism, because these two sacraments together make up Christian initiation.

But I fear that the new converts would be overwhelmed by two sacraments administered at the same time—both mentally and psysically—it seems better if after some time, they become conscious of their Christian vocation [by which he means confirmation] on another occasion. Therefore the administration of confirmation is not prescribed immediately after baptism, but the possibility might be allowed.[16]

This quote shows the tenor of discussion on the sacraments of baptism and confirmation. It seems that the distinction between baptized and nonbaptized persons seeking to join the church was not clearly defined or understood.[17] To take the Cardinal's observation and prepare a shortened ritual of adult baptism would be to obscure again the fact that many protestant churches' baptisms are valid. Cardinal Alfrink also argues against the joining of confirmation with the rite, at least in the practice of giving it together with baptism.

This is a very cautious approach, recognizing the principle that baptism and confirmation belong together, fearful of "overwhelming" the new convert. He does allow, however, the possibility of confirmation being given immediately after baptism, presumably by the bishop or priest who baptized. It is obvious that he is hesitant about the reception of converts, seeing a shortened ritual of the catechumenate for baptized persons seeking to join the church (thus calling for conditional baptism). It is a minor point, yet in his words offering the "possibility of confirmation immediately after baptism," he gave evidence of a cautious approach to what must have been an unimaginable change for the cardinals formed in a tradition where only bishops confirmed: conceding to presbyters the faculty to confirm. Cardinal Frings also makes some observations on the catechumenate, noting that it does not make sense for his church because the long ritual foreseen in the text would only make it more difficult for those who wish to join the church.[18]

After the many diverse opinions were discussed, the draft of the document on the liturgy was considered, amended and approved by the members of the Central Commission. With the Commission's approval and the approval of the Holy Father, this document, along with others that had been approved, were sent to all the bishops of the world in preparation for the beginning of the Council.[19]

The Council

At the second General Congregation of the first session of the Council on 16 October 1962, after the counsel of many bishops and members of the presidency was heard, the decision was announced to examine first the draft on the Sacred Liturgy.[20] In the document on the Sacred Liturgy titled simply, *Schema constitutionis de sacra liturgia,* the order for supplying what was omitted in baptism is mentioned in paragraph 53. In the final draft of the constitution, this is paragraph 69. In the draft presented to the council fathers, this section reads

> 53. In place of the ritual for supplying ceremonies for baptized infants, a new rite should be drawn up which signifies the reception of the children into the Church. Similarly, a rite should be drawn up for the newly converted who have been already validly baptized.[21]

General Congregations XIII and XIV on 6 and 7 November 1962, were taken up with the discussion of chapter III of *De sacra liturgia,* "The Sacraments and

Sacramentals," of which the paragraph above is a part. Of 41 interventions on this chapter, 2 make reference to this ritual in the oral presentations; in the written observations, 6 refer to this rite.

Bishop Bekkers, bishop of s'Hertzogenbosch, offered an intervention in the name of the bishops of Holland.[22] He suggested a change to indicate that the newly converted is being perfectly integrated into the church of Christ (i.e., the perfection of that which was begun in their baptism).[23] Bishop Van Bekkum of Ruteng, Indonesia, making an intervention in the name of 24 Indonesian bishops and 15 others, asked for an approach to all the sacraments within a more general comment on the entire *Rituale Romanum*. He asked that the *Rituale Romanum* be arranged so that the rite "for those coming" to the Catholic faith can be celebrated with the community surrounding "those joining."[24]

In the written observations, one bishop saw no need at all for this paragraph and suggested omitting it.[25] Bishop Carli of Segni wrote an insightful reflection seeing some ambiguity and danger in the linking of infants and adults in this paragraph. He notes the ambiguity that may be seen here in comparing the validly baptized with the case of infants baptized in emergency. Further, he saw a danger that the title of the rite ("for the reception of infants into the church") could be the occasion for the erroneous opinion that these children, already baptized, are not yet part of the church. He proposed a clarification to separate the two different groups. He suggested placing the issue of the infants already baptized together with the article about infant baptism, and the issue of adults validly baptized in a separate paragraph.[26]

Bishop Fares of Catanzaro and Squillace in Italy was concerned that the text made no reference to a renunciation of heresy.[27] Bishop S. László of Eisenstadt in Austria suggested an addition in the rubrics of the new rite to help judge the validity of the non-Catholic baptism.[28]

Bishop McEleney of Kingston, Jamaica, emphasized that care should be taken that there be no confusion in the ritual between the reception of those validly baptized and rebaptism. He suggested also eliminating the terminology *supplendi omissa* (for supplying what has been omitted) in the title.[29]

From these interventions, both spoken and written, there are a number of issues that come to the fore. First, a question for many is the validity of baptism. It is worthy of note that even with pronouncements from the Holy See acknowledging the validity of baptism administered in various protestant churches, questions remained in the minds of the bishops. Another problem in the text is the linking of two different groups; infants already baptized and adults validly baptized in other Christian traditions. A third issue raised is the need for a communal celebration. Both in the case of the infants and the adults, the bishops asked for a public celebration of the rites.

When the second session of Vatican II convened in October of 1963, Archbishop Paul Hallinan (Atlanta) was selected to explain the revisions of chapter III, now titled "On the Other Sacraments and the Sacramentals," to the assembled bishops in General Congregation XLVIII on 15 October 1963. He explained that all the statements and observations, both oral and written, of the council fathers were carefully taken into account by the Liturgical Commission and its subcommissions. Some observations had been treated in other amendments, some were referred to other commissions of the council; others that were too detailed were referred to a (yet to be established) postconciliar commission. This left the amendments that affected the constitution.

Although Archbishop Hallinan had only a few words to say about the paragraph we are studying (number 69 in the reworked document), the changes and explanation show that the comments of the bishops were taken into account. Suggestions were accepted to clarify the purpose of these rites. The changes made to the second part of the paragraph, dealing with the reception of adults, "are made to better signify the nature of the reception of the newly converted."[30] In addition, the revised paragraph calls not for a *similar* rite but for a *new* rite by which they are admitted to full communion, although no clear indications are given of what this rite might look like.

A final text of chapter III was offered to the body of bishops for their approval in this congregation, and it was approved with a vote of 2,107 fathers for approval and 35 negative.[31] The entire text of the schema, now known as *Sacrosanctum concilium* (Constitution on the Sacred Liturgy) was definitively approved and promulgated on 4 December 1963, with a final vote of 2,147 bishops for and 4 against.[32]

To help understand paragraph 69 and the climate in which it was formed, some commentary may be helpful. A commentary on the text of the Constitution on the Sacred Liturgy notes that this paragraph

> is intended to make up for the incongruity which is manifested in the fact that a child who has received private baptism is subjected almost in a mechanical way to the ceremonies he had been deprived of, including all the exorcisms, so that the impression could be gained that the child was still in the grip of the devil. What in the new act is to be added to the private baptism, is the visible and public form of reception in the Church. Similar is the case of the convert who is baptized and wishes to be received fully into the Church. For this case the liturgical books had so far not contained any generally valid rite, except the one contained in the recent editions of the *Pontificale Romanum* and the rite for release from excommunication in the *Rituale Romanum,* in which vestiges of public repentance before the Church live on. Here too the creation of an appropriate form is a long-felt need.[33]

There was no rite at the time of the Council. The law for those days was contained in canon 2314 §2, and in the response of the Holy Office of 20 July 1859, "only the abjuration or profession of faith is received followed by the absolution from censures."[34] From the tradition, it is clear that an imposition of hands was used in the early church to restore people to communion. The traditional gesture, however, dropped out of the ritual that was in use (at least in the United States) at the time of the Council.

Other Conciliar Documents

Decree on Eastern Churches

Orientalium Ecclesiarum, the Decree on Eastern Churches, serves as an important guide to relations with the Eastern Christians. One paragraph of this document will have a direct influence on the new *ordo:*

> 25. Nothing more than what a simple profession of the Catholic faith requires should be asked of people of separated eastern churches coming into the unity of the Catholic church under the influence of the grace of the Holy Spirit. And since the valid priesthood has been preserved among them, eastern clerics joining the Catholic church may exercise their own orders in accordance with the norms established by the competent authority.[35]

This is new. There is a resonance here from the Acts of the Apostles 15:28: "For it has seemed good to the Holy Spirit and to us to impose on you no further burden than these essentials."[36]

Dogmatic Constitution on the Church

Lumen Gentium, the dogmatic Constitution on the Church, also speaks of the gift of baptism, and the communion which is shared by all the baptized.

> 15. For several reasons the church recognizes that it is joined to those who, though baptized and so honored with the Christian name, do not profess the faith in its entirety or do not preserve the unity of communion under the successor of Peter. For there are many who hold the sacred scripture in honor as the norm for believing and living, and display a sincere religious

zeal. They lovingly believe in God the almighty Father and in Christ, the Son of God and Savior. They are marked by baptism, by which they are joined to Christ; and indeed there are other sacraments that they recognize and accept in their own churches or ecclesiastical communities. . . . In addition to this, there is a communion in prayers and other spiritual benefits. Indeed there is a true bond in the holy Spirit, since it is he who is also at work in these persons with his sanctifying power through gifts and graces, and he has strengthened some of them to the point of the shedding of their blood. In this way the Spirit arouses in all of Christ's disciples desire and action so that all may be peacefully united, in the way established by Christ, in one flock under one shepherd.[37]

This shows a development in the tradition. Baptism is recognized as our common bond, even if a full communion is not shared. This is part of the tradition. That the Holy Spirit is recognized as working outside the communion of the church is a significant move in the traditional position.[38]

Decree on Ecumenism
Unitatis Redintegratio, the Decree on Ecumenism, must also be taken into account, inasmuch as it speaks of baptism. Although the following excerpts did not necessarily have a direct influence on the formation of the *ordo,* these few words indicate the mind of the council fathers in their attitudes toward ecumenism and baptism.

3. . . . Those who are now born into these communities and who are brought up in the faith of Christ cannot be accused of the sin involved in the separation, and the Catholic church looks upon them as sisters and brothers, with respect and love. For those who believe in Christ and have been truly baptized are in some kind of communion with the catholic church, even though this communion is imperfect. . . . [39]

4. However, it should be evident that, when individuals wish for full catholic communion, their preparation and reconciliation is an undertaking which of its nature is distinct from ecumenical action. But there is no opposition between the two, since each proceeds from the marvelous providence of God.[40]

While this document is directed toward the union of all Christians, it perhaps helped set the tone for the drawing up of the new *ordo,* especially in that no longer is it considered sinful to be born and baptized in "heresy." The church's teaching on baptism is also stated emphatically:

> 22. Whenever the sacrament of baptism is duly administered as our Lord instituted it, and is received with the right dispositions, a person is truly incorporated into the crucified and glorified Christ, and reborn to a sharing of the divine life, as the apostle says: "You were buried together with him in baptism, in which you were also raised with him through faith in the working of God, who raised him from the dead." (Colossians 2:12)
>
> Thus baptism establishes a sacramental bond of unity existing among all who have been reborn by it. But of itself, baptism is only a beginning, an inauguration wholly directed towards the acquisition of the fullness of life in Christ. Baptism therefore, is oriented towards the complete profession of faith, complete incorporation into the institution of salvation such as Christ willed it to be, and finally the completeness of unity which eucharistic communion gives.[41]

This renews the church's constant teaching since antiquity on baptism. In its fullness, baptism is the sacramental bond of unity. It is from baptism that all Christians are called to die and rise with Christ.[42]

The First Ecumenical Directory

Ad totam ecclesiam, the First Ecumenical Directory, was promulgated in 1967 as an aid to responding to ecumenical questions that were raised in the years after the Council. Several excerpts from this important ecumenical document are included to articulate further the Catholic church's attitude toward the issues surrounding the admission of the validly baptized into full communion.

> 12. There can be no doubt cast upon the validity of baptism as conferred among separated Eastern Christians. It is enough therefore to establish the fact that baptism was administered.

Since in the Eastern Churches the sacrament of confirmation (chrism) is always lawfully administered by the priest at the same time as baptism, it often happens that no mention is made of the confirmation in the canonical testimony of baptism. This does not give grounds for doubting that the sacrament was conferred.[43]

14. Indiscriminate conditional baptism of all who desire full communion with the Catholic Church cannot be approved. The sacrament of baptism cannot be repeated (canon 732, 1), and therefore to baptize again conditionally is not allowed unless there is prudent doubt of the fact, or of the validity, of a baptism already administered. (Trent, session VII, can. 4; canon 732, 2)[44]

15. It may happen that after a thorough investigation of a baptism's right administration it is necessary to administer it again conditionally. In due recognition of the teaching that there is only one baptism, the minister is (a.) to properly explain both the reasons why in this case he is baptizing conditionally and the significance of the rite of administration; (b.) to use the nonsolemn rite of baptism.

19. The Decree on Ecumenism makes clear that the brethren born and baptized outside the visible communion of the Catholic Church should be carefully distinguished from those who, though baptized in the Catholic Church, have knowingly and publicly abjured her faith. According to the decree (n. 3) "one cannot charge with the sin of separation those who at present are born into these communities and in them are brought up in the faith of Christ." Hence, in the absence of such blame, if they freely wish to embrace the Catholic faith, they have no need to be absolved from excommunication, but after making profession of their faith according to the regulations set down by the ordinary of the place they should be admitted to the full communion of the Catholic Church. What Canon 2314 prescribes is only applicable to those who, after culpably giving up the Catholic faith or communion, repent and ask to be reconciled with mother Church.[45]

20. What has just been said of absolution from censures obviously applies for the same reason to the abjuring of heresy.[46]

This Directory was promulgated at the same time as the *ordo* was under consideration by the *Consilium*. As can be seen in the above excerpts, the implications for the celebration of the reception of converts are evident. These remarks seem to be directed toward the *ordo* that was under consideration. This Directory will have a strong influence on the shape of the new rite.

Summation

This chapter has unfolded the Conciliar discussion calling for a new *ordo*. The presentation has included the ante-preparatory and preparatory period of the Council as well as the floor discussion, the final text and some commentary on *Sacrosanctum concilium,* 69. The entire study is useful since it provides background and insight into the thoughts and hopes of the council fathers from the initial days of preparation to the end of Vatican II.

Also presented briefly are other pertinent documents from the Council. The Decree on the Eastern Churches makes clear reference to what is required for full communion for those coming from the separated Eastern churches. The Dogmatic Constitution on the Church reiterates the church's position on baptism. The Decree on Ecumenism is noted because it recalls the church's understanding and acceptance of the baptism conferred in many protestant churches. Without directly affecting the content of the new *ordo,* these documents definitely influenced the atmosphere of ecumenical sensitivity in which the new *ordo* was composed.

Finally, a postconciliar document was presented. This First Ecumenical Directory sets forth exact guidelines for the position of the church in accepting people into full communion as this document was issued at the same time as this *ordo* was being conceived. Our investigation turns now to the process of drawing up the new *ordo*.

Chapter 5

The Post-Conciliar Development of the Ritual

■

The history of the ritual treatment of the reconciliation/reception of the validly baptized into the full communion of the church has been presented. Now this study will sketch the lines of development of the new *ordo* in the work of the Consilium following Vatican II. Shortly after the promulgation of the Constitution on the Sacred Liturgy, *Sacrosanctum concilium* (SC), Pope Paul VI established the Consilium for the implementation of the Constitution and gave some norms from the Constitution to be put into effect immediately.[1]

In early 1965, the Consilium prepared an Instruction on the Implementation of the Constitution on the Sacred Liturgy *(Inter Oecumenici)*.[2] Its purpose was to articulate the functions of the episcopal conferences in the liturgical reform, and also to explain more fully the principles that would guide the reform.[3] It is organized following the outline of the Constitution. The section dealing with baptism lists the elements that are to be omitted from the Rite of Supplying Ceremonies for a person already baptized (SC, 69). A number of exorcisms (of which there had been four) were dropped immediately.

The work of the reform of the *Rituale Romanum* (RR) was assigned to study groups XXII and XXIII of the Consilium.[4] The general principles to be followed for this reform were delineated by Balthasar Fischer.[5] An important principle in the preparation of the new RR was its relation to particular rituals. It was noted that the RR of 1614, promulgated by Pope Paul V, was never imposed on the Latin church and that, in fact, the rituals of some particular churches had been used down to recent times. Adaptation by the local churches was seen as necessary, "so long as the substantial unity of the Roman Rite would be preserved" (SC, 38). Particular rituals would be developed by the local ordinary or the episcopal conference. The development of the Latin typical edition *(editio typica)* was perceived as most important because from it would flow the adaptations that help the sacramental celebrations come alive for the universal church. The introductory notes *(praenotanda)* that were added to the RR following the Council of Trent would be rewritten and deepened to include the theological developments of Vatican II. These instructions may be adapted in particular rituals and should bring out the ecclesial nature of the sacraments. The following points were to be emphasized in the process:

- Communal celebration is preferred (SC, 27).

- Active participation of the people should be provided for in the rubrics (SC, 30 and 31).

- No distinction for private persons or conditions will be accepted (SC, 32).

- The rites should be simple and not need explaining (SC, 34).

- Reading of Sacred Scripture should be abundantly used (SC, 35, 1).

- The proper place for the sermon and/or instruction should be noted (SC, 35, 2–3).

Fischer further details the work and lists a schema of the work that needs to be done directly following the lines of the Constitution on the Sacred Liturgy, paragraphs 64–71. The declarations (explanatory notes) are included from the preconciliar draft. Fischer and Pierre-Marir Gy note that this rite should be drawn up with the counsel of the Secretariat for Christian Unity.[6]

An early letter to the consultors of the study group asks for their observations on a number of questions, including: "How do we envision the conditional baptism (if necessary) of catechumens coming from the churches separated from Rome?"[7] Unfortunately, any written replies or accounts of the discussion of these questions are not available. We can note here, however, the use of equivocal language, since those "coming to Rome" who may need conditional baptism are referred to as *catechumens,* the same as the unbaptized. This linguistic slip in the question shows an undercurrent in the discussion about those "coming to Rome," which will gradually be completely rearticulated in the process of drafting the new order.[8]

First Schema

The work of the Consilium is documented in a series of *schemata,* which are records of the discussion leading to the new rituals. Work began at a meeting in 1967.[9] The third item discussed at this meeting was the Rite of Admission to the Communion of the Church. The minutes of the meeting begin with the account of a lively discussion over the interpretation that should be given in paragraph 19 of the recently published First Ecumenical Directory.

> According to the decree, "Those who are now born into these communities and who are brought up in the faith of Christ cannot be accused of the sin involved in the separation, . . . no absolution from excommunication is done, but only a profession of faith, *according to the norms established by the local Ordinary,* for their admission into the full communion of the Catholic Church.[10]

The meaning of the italicized phrase is unclear. To what is it linked? Does the ordinary determine the norms concerning the profession of faith, or determine the general norms for admitting people into full communion with the church (some even thought this may include drawing up an *ordo*)? Fischer would ask for an interpretation about this.

The discussion of the ritual followed. Examples were presented along with some proposals. Theological and pastoral principles were considered, and finally the liturgical structure of the *ordo* was sketched out. The members of the study group discussed the need for two rituals: a solemn rite and an abbreviated rite.

In the first part of the discussion, two rites were presented from a protestant church in Germany. One of these rites was celebrated within the "divine service" and one took place outside the "divine service." Next, a structure proposed by Frederick McManus was presented:

- The profession of faith is given in front of the community or with the community.

- The rite of confirmation (if it is done).

- The sign of peace or some other sign.

- When possible, the admission should happen during Mass, and holy communion should be offered under both species.

- Mention should be made by the celebrant in the homily and mention should be made of the godparents in the prayers of the faithful.[11]

Jacques Cellier, a French priest, presented the practice of the church of Lyons that he had experienced at a catechumenal institute there. The ritual of admission was inserted into the Easter celebration. Cellier outlined the distinction of three different types of people, all validly baptized, who sought to be received into the church: those who have only accepted baptism, not true initiation into heresy; those who accepted baptism and initiation, but who gradually and with time have abandoned the practice of their religion; and those who at length were baptized, initiated and had a long practice of their faith. Each of the three distinct groups had a different formula for their reception into the church.

An objection was raised that with the profession of faith being made in the community with the renewal of baptismal promises in common as at the Easter Vigil would be, in a certain sense, anonymous. This was not seen as a problem since the public element of the rite then would be eucharistic communion. Any of the things that need to be done privately (e.g., conditional baptism, confession, individual profession of faith) could be done in a small group. It was also pointed out that with the restoration of the catechumenate these elements would be able to be dealt with in other ways.

Theological and pastoral principles were discussed. The suggestion was made that the process of preparing baptized people to be received could develop along the lines of the newly restored catechumenate. There was a strong reaction against this idea, in light of new ecumenical attitudes. Also, it was argued, a preparation period of a long duration would not be necessary, especially in a communal and public way.

Suggestions were put forward to celebrate the admission into full communion in the context of the Easter Vigil. In this way baptism would be clearly understood as the sacrament of unity. Those to be received already share a certain unity (albeit imperfect) with the church, and this comes to fruition (perfection) with the celebration of confirmation and eucharist. A final point in this discussion noted that attention must be given to the texts of the orations and the profession of faith with regard to whether the person is from the separated oriental churches or from the separated protestant churches.

A suggestion was made that the liturgy of the word would be important to stress in this rite, since all the Christian churches agreed on the importance of the word of God. A proposal was made to present a Book of the Gospels *(evangelarium)* to those being received. This idea received strong negative reaction. It was argued that these people are already Christian; they have heard and know the gospel of Christ very well.

The preparation of the profession of faith would need to include the Secretariat for Christian Unity and the Congregation for the Doctrine of the Faith. The possibility of various formulas adapted to the different life circumstances of the persons was discussed.

The consultors had a lengthy discussion about the traditional gesture of the imposition of hands. Some felt that this gesture was too closely related to the gesture for absolution in the new rite of penance and confirmation. The gesture would serve here as an act of admission into (reconciliation with) the church as well as a gesture of forgiveness of sins.[12] Solutions to the problem were proposed: Use only one hand for this gesture; two hands then would be imposed for confirmation. A consultor who was working on the rite of penance noted that the laying on of two hands signifies absolution. What should be done when confirmation is given in the same celebration? One possible solution would be to impose two hands for the act of admission and absolution; then the celebrant would prolong the imposition of one hand while he prayed the prayer for confirmation.

A strong point was made for the conferral of confirmation by the minister who would receive the person into full communion. Even though few priests had the faculty to confirm, it was considered most fitting for the confirmation to happen at the same celebration, with the community that witnessed the reception.

A strong suggestion also was made to pay attention to the prayer texts. The profession of faith would need to be accepted by the celebrant, but the community, too, would have a role. There should be some way for the community to give thanks and offer its prayers; this could happen in the prayers of the faithful. Another suggestion for communal involvement and public celebration was a proposal to develop some sort of "catechumenate" for these people coming to the church.

The discussion of the study group moved next to the liturgical organization of the *ordo*. The ritual text would begin by describing the first type of celebration, which would be outside Mass. This would begin with a liturgy of the word with appropriate songs for the celebration. A homily was prescribed, then the actual admission to full communion with the following structure:

- Profession of faith

- Imposition of hands

- Confirmation (if it is to be done)

- Concluding prayer: prayers of the faithful including prayers of thanks and prayers for perseverance[13]

It is then noted that if the admission is celebrated in Mass, the liturgy of the eucharist follows and holy communion is given to the newly received under both species.

An abbreviated order would not include a liturgy of the word. The celebrant would begin with an admonition taken from the gospel. Then the structure proposed above follows with the profession of faith, imposition of hands and the general intercessions from the community. In the Latin text of Schema 236, the roles of the minister (prayer with the imposition of hands), the candidate (profession of faith) and the community (prayers of the faithful) are most clearly distinguished.[14]

General Principles and First Outline of the Rite

A summary of the discussion on the rite of admission was written, comprising general principles and a first outline of the rite.[15] The general principles of the rite are summarized as follows:[16]

> 1. Following *Sacrosanctum concilium,* 26, the admission should be a "celebration of the church," thus a communal celebration whether in the Mass or outside Mass.

> 2. This ritual should be linked with the paschal mystery; indeed, the annual celebration of Easter is most opportune to celebrate the rite. Thus, Lent would be an excellent time for the final preparation of the candidates for full communion.

> 3. The order of admission completes the initiation begun in baptism; indeed, if possible, it should be linked with the conferral of confirmation and eucharistic participation. If the one admitted is from the Orthodox (who already have valid sacraments of initiation), mention should be made of the initiation already completed as the foundation of admission.

> 4. For the admission of one born and baptized outside the communion of the Catholic church, (Ecumenical Directory, 19), the abjurations from heresy are no longer required (Ecumenical Directory, 20), but "according to the norms of the local ordinary" (Ecumenical Directory, 19), he or she makes the profession of faith with the adaptations according to the respective circumstances to be determined by the Secretariat for Christian Unity.

The first outline of the rite is summarized as follows:

1. If the admission is done outside of the Mass, it is preceded by a liturgy of the word with a homily by the celebrant.

2. At the end of the homily, the celebrant invites the one to be received *(admittendus)* to confess the faith. In this introductory admonition, he [the celebrant] makes mention with thanksgiving of the baptism already received, as it is the foundation of admission.

3. The profession of faith follows.

4. Then, the celebrant, imposing both hands on the head of the one to be received, pronounces the formula, which at the same time expresses admission into the church and remission of sins (which the *admittendus* has confessed before, privately to the celebrant.) Thus, it should clearly appear that the admission is not to be identified with the remission of sins: however, personal sins are remitted by the admission.

5. It is proper that the celebrant, even if he is only a priest, be permitted to receive the candidate and, if possible, be allowed to confirm immediately. The rite of confirmation begins with the extension of hands and concludes with the chrismation.

6. The rite of admission is completed with the universal prayers, which begin with prayers of thanksgiving, and in the first place intercessions with prayers for perseverance for the newly received.

7. If the reception is celebrated during the Mass, the Mass follows in which holy communion is offered to the newly received under both species (according to the Instruction on the Worship of the Eucharist 32/1).

8. If on account of circumstances the joining of the admission with the liturgy of the word seems less opportune, the celebration will begin with an **67**

exhortation to the celebration, which takes its origin from a word of Sacred Scripture.

Frederick McManus offered a detailed critique of this first proposal.[17] He argued strongly that preference should be given in every case to celebration within Mass, and insists "emphasis in the rite is upon reception into full and visible communion, . . . reception into the eucharistic community." Reception outside Mass should be the exception. In no way is this rite a baptism, and it should not look like one. Baptism is the "basis of the unity already existing and . . . the present celebration is rather an admission to communion of a person hitherto separated or not in full communion." The profession of faith is the "condition which every member of the eucharistic assembly undergoes before admission to communion." There should be no suggestion of a relationship between admission to communion and forgiveness or remission of sins.

He questions the desire to link this reception with the annual celebration of Easter, since "in the past this reception into communion has been treated as a 'conversion' with its own kind of catechumenate." In the United States, it would be important to see the rite in light of its ecumenical concerns. Any elements of the rite "that would cast doubt upon the baptism of other Christians which has been properly celebrated or upon the religious life they have been leading prior to their reception into communion" must be avoided. Similarly, he suggests avoiding all discussion of the "validity or non-validity of the eucharist in various" churches. He suggests that no reference be made at all to this matter.

McManus suggests that the *ordo* should be sufficiently adaptable so it can be used not only for public, communal celebrations, but also for a smaller, private celebration of this reception, according to the temperament of the person.

McManus raised questions about the symbolism of the imposition of hands:

> It seems to me to be entirely impossible not to identify the act of admission with the forgiveness of sins if the imposition of hands is the single sign of these two. It is, moreover, not clear to me why there must be a public remission of sins in these circumstances; if there ever is an occasion for private confession and absolution, it is this—when the intent of the new rite is to avoid judging whether the person has been guilty in the act of separation from the Church.

McManus suggests using a different sign for the reception, such as the kiss of peace.

He agrees that confirmation should follow immediately, given by the minister who received the person, and also is in agreement that holy communion should be offered under both forms. In the prayers of the faithful, he questions the idea of praying for perseverance of the individual: "In the circumstances this would appear patronizing and embarrassing." He suggests adding "a prayer for unity and prayer for the forgiveness of sins against unity, whether they are committed by the Roman Catholic community or by others."

A Second Proposal

During the same period, the U.S. Bishops' Committee on the Liturgy as well as the Bishops' Committee on Ecumenical and Interreligious Affairs (NCCB) were developing a proposal for the Reception of Baptized Christians into Full Communion with the Catholic Church. It is not clear if the Bishops' Committee on the Liturgy was preparing this *ordo* for the church in the United States, or if it was preparing this proposal for the use of the Consilium.[18]

The proposal suggests that the reception into the community take place at the Sunday eucharist of the community (SC, 26). It is also suggested that this "public and communal" celebration be continued after the liturgy with some sort of informal, social gathering of the community.

A record of the reception into full communion would need to be made, making note of the earlier baptism in another church. For the profession of faith, the Apostles' Creed or the Nicene Creed could be used, or the question format for the renewal of baptismal promises, or one of the forms from the *Collectio Rituum* could be used without the words of abjuration (Cf. First Ecumenical Directory, 20).

McManus insisted that those coming to the church already baptized should in no way be equated with catechumens. These people may have need of basic Christian instruction, but the fact of their baptism changes their status in the eyes of the church. If the earlier baptism is reasonably in doubt, the person should be baptized conditionally, in private.

McManus noted that the *ordo* should not be construed in any way as "conversion to Christian faith and should not resemble Christian initiation." The abjuration of heresy and absolution from excommunication are to be dropped. The Ecumenical Directory modifies the prescriptions of canon 2314 and replaces the rite observed in this country for more than a century (Instruction, 20 July 1859). Only a profession of faith is required. The local ordinary is permitted to develop regulations for reception into full communion.

The proposal of the Consilium spoke of two different rites, one more solemn and one abbreviated. The more solemn rite would take place in the context of the Sunday Mass. In the homily or after the homily, the priest could say some words of welcome to the Christian and introduce him or her to the community expressing "the reception into full and visible communion with the Catholic Church."

The profession of faith could be recited by the Christian alone, using the Apostles' Creed, or said with the community, using the Nicene Creed. The prayers of the faithful should include one or more petitions for the individual and for the unity of the church. Some form of the kiss of peace is suggested as the gesture for welcoming the individual "at the customary time." The person would receive holy communion under both kinds.

An abbreviated ritual would be prepared for particular situations. Pastoral discretion would be allowed in choosing the proper venue for the celebration of the rite according to the "background or temperament of the individual." For some, a solemn public reception may not be opportune or possible. In these cases, a shorter rite is suggested: "It is suitable to precede the profession of faith with a reading from Scripture and words of welcome and reception and to follow the profession of faith with some form of prayer of the faithful and the Lord's Prayer."

Three bishops' reactions (mostly positive) to this proposal were found in the archives of the Bishops' Committee on the Liturgy. One shows high sensitivity to the ecumenical implications of this rite; he suggests a more prominent placement of the remarks about the clear distinction that is to be made between catechumens and baptized Christians desiring full communion; and if the person is to be conditionally baptized, this should be done privately, before the public celebration of reception.[19] Another bishop finds a problem with the fact that the person will not have a chance to make a sacramental confession before receiving communion.[20] The question was also raised regarding the immediate conferral of confirmation which "might theoretically be desirable to show the complement of confirmation to baptism but impractical in present church discipline where so few priests have the faculty to confirm."[21]

There is no clear indication what purpose this work was intended to serve. The fact that McManus was a part of study group XXIII of the Consilium working on this *ordo* offers the clue that these proposals and reactions would help him in his role as a consultor to the Consilium.

Second Schema

In Schema 252 (3 November 1967) the first formal outline of the rite is presented.[22] It delineates the process of the work, the principles used and the first outline of the rite.

A change in language used to describe the rite is found here. Instead of the terminology from *Sacrosanctum concilium,* 69, a new set of terms is adopted, following the lead of the Ecumenical Dirctory and the inspiration of the Decree on the Eastern Churches.[23] Rather than a "rite for converts who have already been validly baptized," the second schema refers to a "rite for the admission of the already validly baptized into the full communion of the Catholic Church."

The sketch of the rite drawn up after the first meeting in Trier, Germany, was sent to all the consultors of study groups XXII and XXIII for their observations. After seeing these observations (especially those of F. McManus) the entire sketch had to be thoroughly reworked. The observations of the consultors were taken into account along with the counsel of P. Arrighi of the Secretariat for Christian Unity.

In the first paragraph it is noted that a doubt had arisen about this new rite after the publication of the First Ecumenical Directory (14 May 1967). The Secretariat for Christian Unity clarified the phrase, "according to the norms established by the local ordinary."[24] (Some had interpreted this phrase to mean that local ordinaries could draw up an *ordo* for use in their dioceses, and some experimentation had already begun. Others had interpreted the phrase to mean that Ordinaries could draw up a profession of faith.) It "means the bishop can institute norms for catechetical preparation, he can concede public or private celebrations, and he can enact statutes about how the event is to be recorded in the proper books."[25] Also, it is noted that according to *Sacrosanctum concilium*, 63b, the episcopal conferences have the possibility of adapting the *ordo* to the particular needs of a region or country.

The second paragraph declares that the rite needs to appear as a celebration of the church and should have its culmination in eucharistic communion (SC, 26). The admission should take place within the Mass. Any appearances of triumphalism should be avoided. With renewed concern for ecumenism, this was no doubt suggested by the Secretariat for Christian Unity. At times it will be more proper to celebrate the rite in a smaller celebration among friends; at other times, it could be celebrated outside Mass. In such a case, the person should soon have the opportunity to participate in a celebration of the Mass and join in eucharistic communion. The possibility is suggested that this celebration take place as part of the Paschal Vigil; in such way, the reception would be clearly linked with the paschal mystery.

For the reception, "the brethren born and baptized outside the visible communion of the Catholic Church" are only required to make a profession of faith. The abjuration of heresy was not to be required.[26] The conferral of confirmation should be inserted in the celebration. This should be the case especially if the reception happens as part of the Mass and if the newly received has not already been validly confirmed. The celebrant, even if a presbyter, should be able to confirm the newly received.[27] The sponsors, family and spouse, with catechesis, could be offered holy communion under both species.

Schema 252 also included a suggestion of what the ritual might look like in outline form. A somewhat complicated process was detailed for what would happen when the reception would be celebrated in the Mass. **73**

First, the person should confess to a confessor of his or her choosing after having told the priest of the forthcoming reception. A special form of absolution would be drawn up that recognized the fact that the reception was soon to take place. The individual can then receive communion immediately after being received, and the connection between the reception and eucharistic communion would be evident to the Catholic faithful.[28]

A sponsor should take part in the ritual of reception and would be the person who had accompanied the candidate in the preparation for admission to full communion. The schema also presented the unfolding of the *ordo* within the particular celebration. After the homily the celebrant invites the candidate to come forward with the sponsor and to make the profession of faith. In this introductory admonition, gratitude should be expressed to God for those validly baptized who are now to be admitted into full communion.

The Creed for the profession of faith would be the Nicene-Constantinople Creed, proclaimed together with the community. The one to be received would add a brief phrase at the end of the Creed that may be something like: I believe and profess all that the Holy Catholic Church believes and teaches. It was also foreseen that the Creed could be done in the question form used at the Easter Vigil. The convert would respond with the rest of the people to the questions of the Creed. The convert alone responds to the final question, Do you believe and profess all that the Holy Catholic Church believes and teaches?

Paragraph 13 dealt with the gesture of admission.

> To signify the admission, according to the ancient practice which is foreseen in the *Roman Pontifical,* Part III for reconciliation, the imposition of the hand should be employed.[29] The celebrant lays his right hand on the head of the candidate for reception and says: "I admit you into full communion of the Catholic Church." Then, he takes the hands of the candidate

into his hands (or if it is permitted, he embraces the candidate).[30] With the permission of the ordinary of the place, this gesture, depending on local and other circumstances, can be substituted with another, which similarly expresses friendship and acceptance.[31]

The ritual gesture of admission foreseen here is an imposition of the hand on the head of the candidate with some ritual words. Then, a gesture of peace (or welcome) is made by the celebrant to the candidate. That the rite of reconciliation from the *Pontificale Romanum* is mentioned reveals that this ritual was envisioned as somehow penitential.

Paragraph 14 proposed another way of admission.

> But, if the person admitted is not yet confirmed and the bishop (or priest having the faculty of confirming) is admitting, he immediately confirms the candidate with a brief adapted rite and so, with one and the same imposition of (one) hand, he admits/receives and confirms with the following formula being placed before the confirmation formula: "I admit you into full communion of the Catholic Church." In this case, the greeting spoken of in no. 13 is done after confirmation.[32]

The wording of this proposal has implications for the preceding paragraph. The first phrase, "if the person admitted is not yet confirmed," presumes a candidate may be already validly confirmed (from an Eastern church). If confirmation is to take place, the act of reception happens immediately before the sacramental confirmation; thus one imposition of hands has two meanings (i.e., reception and confirmation). A greeting as mentioned in the preceding paragraph is also given.

The general intercessions are indicated and follow the reception even if it is celebrated outside Mass. In the introduction to these prayers, thanksgiving is expressed; the newly received is mentioned at the beginning of the intercessions. Paragraph 16 directs that the entire assembly would greet the newly received. "After the prayers the sponsor or sponsors, and the others if not too numerous, may greet the newly received person in the way the celebrant greeted him [or her]."[33] Finally, the outline of the ritual indicates that holy communion is to be offered under both species to the newly received.

Brief mention is given of what should happen if the celebration would take place outside Mass and outside a liturgy of the word.

> The celebration should begin with an admonition by the celebrant, which is adapted from the Sacred Scriptures in which for example, the greatness of the mercy of God is mentioned, and the action of God in the person's life who is being received. Mention can also be made of the Eucharistic table, which the newly received will take part in soon.[34]

Third Schema

In Schema 256 (20 November 1967) the second draft of the principles and outline of the *ordo* are presented.[35] Some changes were made merely for linguistic purposes while other interventions, whether changes or additions, were more substantial. Only the substantial modifications will be treated here.

This account of the history of this particular *ordo* is given with only a few elements added. The story notes that some small changes were made in the document after a meeting with Cardinal Bea, president of the Secretariat for Christian Unity. A meeting of the *relators* ("reporters") of the Consilium on November 17 produced other changes. It is also noted that a Swiss protestant professor, Rev. Dom. Feine,[36] was consulted about the proposal. He had a favorable reaction to the progress of the work.

The number of paragraphs in this section is the same, with the same general content as the preceding schema. Only a few changes are to be noted here.

The first change is that "if for grave reasons" the reception cannot be celebrated in the Mass, it is to be celebrated in a liturgy of the word. *Sacrosanctum concilium,* 35 is invoked here, which recalls that "[i]n sacred celebrations a more ample, more varied and more suitable reading from sacred scripture should be restored." But this same reception without a proper liturgy of the word cannot be completely excluded. The insistence that the reception take place within the Mass is weakened. It is strongly urged that the celebration take place within at least a liturgy of the word, although this, too, is not absolute. Moreover, in such a celebration, "mention should be made of eucharistic communion as the sign of admission."

In the earlier schema, the Easter Vigil was strongly encouraged as the privileged moment for reception. In this draft that suggestion is weakened: The Paschal Vigil could be the "opportune moment" for the reception of the convert, rather than the "most opportune" time for the celebration, as is noted in the previous schema. Schema 256 presumes more strongly that the reception would be celebrated during the Sunday eucharist, and it was suggested that a special formula for absolution be drawn up for the convert's celebration of the sacrament of penance (this would later be dropped). Also, debate about presbyters having the faculty to confirm in the rite of reception influenced this draft. At the November 1967 meeting the Consilium discussed not only this text, but also the text on the sacrament of confirmation.[37] McManus mentions the anomaly in conceding the faculty of confirmation to the presbyter, but he does in fact support the proposal. He suggested that theological and pastoral solutions be sought that allow confirmation to take its proper position in the celebration of the sacraments of Christian initiation.[38]

In the outline of the ritual, the special formula to be said by the candidate after the Creed was removed because it needed further study. When the reception takes place in the context of a liturgy of the word, the liturgy should conclude with the Lord's Prayer, sung or recited by everyone.[39] This is also suggested as the ending if the reception takes place without a Mass and without a liturgy of the word.

Fourth Schema

Schema 276 (8 March 1968) presents the ritual in almost final form.[40] The members of the Consilium approved the *ordo* with respect to its substance; with their observations the rite was drawn up in the last days of 1967 in a meeting at Le Saulchoir.[41] This was sent to the consultors, and with their observations the rite was definitively edited in February 1968 in a meeting at Trier.[42]

The introductory notes are divided into 11 paragraphs. Because this document was newly drawn up, we will look at each paragraph in detail, noting its relation to Schema 256. This schema is proposed as the form of the ritual and as such it follows a different order than the previous documents.

Paragraph 1 calls for the *ordo* to appear as a celebration of the church, which should have as its high point eucharistic communion; thus, the celebration would take place during the Mass. This paragraph corresponds directly with paragraph 2 in Schema 256 with no substantial changes.

A new paragraph was added for Eastern Christians; its material was not mentioned in any of the previous schemata. It states that "for faithful of the separated oriental churches, who perhaps for some time already have participated in the sacraments of the Catholic Church, the local Ordinary may permit that the reception be done without any special rite."[43] The Decree on Eastern Churches, no. 25 is the basis for this paragraph, along with the First Ecumenical Directory, no. 12.

The general characteristics for the celebration and some criteria for choosing what shape the particular celebration of reception are presented next. It is a more nuanced version of the same material from the earlier schema: Any show of triumphalism should be avoided; therefore, the circumstances of the person being received, as well as the place, should be taken into account. If a solemn celebration with the entire community does not seem opportune, it is possible to celebrate with a smaller group or a group of family and friends. If for grave reasons the Mass cannot be celebrated, the celebration of the rite should take place in the context of at least a liturgy of the word. When even this is not possible, the reception can be celebrated without a liturgy of the word; but in this case at least the order for the reception should be followed. The person being received should be consulted about the form of reception.[44]

If the reception would be celebrated outside the Mass, a celebration of the eucharist should follow soon in which the newly received can participate fully for the first time.[45] In the previous schema, the paragraph that follows calls for a close link of this reception with the paschal mystery, and even celebrating this at the Paschal Vigil as a first option. This idea is totally absent in the *praenotanda* of Schema 276.

Some elements are presented for the first time in this schema. A new addition to the discussion speaks about the preparation needed for reception into full communion. A preparation both "doctrinal and spiritual according to the pastoral needs of each individual" is required for reception. In this instruction, it should be made clear that the person is to be received into the fullness of the paschal mystery.[46] Norms are given (in the Ecumenical Directory) for the candidate's sharing in worship during this time of preparation. Also, a caution is given not to equate this time of preparation in any way with the catechumenate.[47]

Paragraph 6 is similar to paragraph 5 from Schema 256, with only a minor linguistic adjustment. "One who is born and baptized outside the visible communion of the Catholic Church is not required to make an abjuration of heresy, but simply a profession of faith."[48]

Paragraph 7 states that it is the office of the bishop to receive validly baptized Christians into full communion. The bishop can delegate this celebration to a presbyter, who will have the faculty for confirmation in the celebration of the reception.[49] This is taken from paragraph 6 in the previous schema, but it is reworked based on a proposal accepted in the November 1967 meeting of the Consilium.[50] The earlier schema was written with the assumption that only those presbyters to whom the faculty was delegated could confirm.[51]

Paragraph 8 makes provisions for the celebration of penance. This corresponds to paragraph 8 of the prior schema and is substantially different from it. The application of a special absolution formula is dropped, as well as the need to "make the connection" between this and the eucharistic communion to follow. In Schema 276, two elements are added: Any confessor can receive this confession; if a celebration with general absolution is customary, the person could participate in this.[52]

Paragraph 9 of the *praenotanda* is substantially the same as paragraph 9 of the previous schema. It speaks about the use of a sponsor (or sponsors) in the celebration. This would be someone who has actually helped the person during the time of preparation.

Paragraph 10 combines paragraphs 7 and 17 of the previous schema. It gives a broad list of those who are to be offered holy communion under both species: not only the newly received, but also the sponsor(s), parents, spouse (if Catholic) and catechists.

Paragraph 11 notes that it is the duty of the episcopal conferences to draw up norms and adaptations for the reception of Christians into full communion. This element is not mentioned in the earlier drafts as such. It interprets the directives in the First Ecumenical Directory, which say, "After making a profession of their faith according to the regulations set down by the ordinary of the place they should be admitted to the full communion of the Catholic Church."[53]

Paragraph 12 details the celebration: The reception is to take place after the homily in which the "celebrant should express gratitude to God and speak of the baptism (already received) as the basis for reception." After the homily the celebrant will invite the candidate and sponsor(s) forward with words based on the prayer over the gifts from the Solemnity of Corpus Christi.[54] The emphasis is on eucharistic communion, which will soon be shared.

Paragraph 13 continues,

> [T]he one to be received together with the faithful recites the Nicene-Constantinople Creed which is always said in this Mass. After, at the celebrant's invitation, the one to be received adds these words: 'I believe and profess all that the Holy Catholic Church believes to be revealed by God.'[55]

Paragraph 14 is the action of admission. The celebrant is directed to lay his right hand on the head of the one to be received,[56] saying, "Receive Lord, this your servant. . . ."[57] The formula is deprecative, that is, directed to the Lord. This would change in the final schema.

Paragraph 15 describes what happens next if confirmation is not to be celebrated. The celebrant is to take the hands of the newly received as a sign of friendly acceptance. Other gestures may be suggested by the local bishops, according to the customs of the region. If confirmation is to be celebrated, this gesture of acceptance takes place after the confirmation.[58]

Paragraph 16 details the procedure for confirmation. If the celebrant is the bishop or a priest who has been delegated to confirm the candidate, immediately after the profession of faith he imposes hands on the head of the candidate and pronounces the deprecative formula of acceptance: "Receive Lord, this your servant. . . ." The prayer for confirmation follows while the celebrant either imposes a hand or extends his hand over the candidate. The candidate is signed with the chrism, and afterward the celebrant extends a greeting.[59]

The next paragraph describes the general intercessions in great detail.[60] Following the general intercessions, if the group is small, all are invited to greet the newly received person in a friendly way.[61] If this greeting is done here the sign of peace is omitted in the Mass. After this, the one received can return to his place.[62] The Mass continues as usual, and the one received and the other participants mentioned should receive holy communion under both species.[63]

The second *ordo* outlines the celebration of reception into full communion when it takes place outside the Mass. A liturgy of the word is celebrated with the priest vested in alb and stole. He greets all present, and then the celebration begins with (an appropriate song and) a reading from Sacred Scripture followed by a homily.[64]

An admonition precedes the profession of faith in which the eucharistic communion is mentioned. Because this is the full sign of unity, very soon after the reception the newly received should participate in the celebration of the eucharist.[65] The reception follows the liturgy of the word as described in the ritual during Mass. The general intercessions conclude the celebration as already described, followed by the Lord's Prayer, either recited or sung, and the priest's blessing.[66] The sponsor(s) and the others (if the group is small) greet the newly received in a friendly way and all depart in peace.[67]

Paragraph 25 treats the celebration of the sacrament of penance. If the reception is celebrated outside Mass, the newly received can celebrate the sacrament of penance after the reception.[68]

The last paragraph describes what needs to take place in the exceptional case that even a liturgy of the word cannot be celebrated:

> [E]verything is done as above, but the celebration begins with an admonition by the celebrant. This admonition should start with a word from Sacred Scripture (for example, in praise of God's mercy which has led the candidate to full communion) and mention should be made of the eucharistic communion that will soon follow.[69]

The appendix gives an example of what the general intercessions may include. An introduction, six intercessions, a response and a concluding prayer are all detailed. If the celebration takes place outside the Mass, words are given to introduce the Lord's Prayer, which in that case would conclude the intercessions.

The introduction invites the community to enter into thanksgiving to God who has brought this baptized person to full communion, which process was begun in his baptism into Christ and brought to completion by the mercy of God. The intercessions follow, with intentions for perseverance for the newly received; for all Christian believers, that they be confirmed in faith and hope; for all who have a desire for heavenly grace, that they be led to the fullness of truth;[70] for those who do not yet believe in Christ;[71] for the peace of all; and for perseverance for ourselves.

Having dissected Schema 276, we can see that the creative process of preparing a new *ordo* is nearing completion. The "discussion of principles" stage has progressed to the "writing" stage, and now in a final step this study turns to look at the final Schema, which was discussed in the tenth plenary session of the Consilium.[72]

Final Schema

Schema 290 (21 April 1968) begins with the history recounted as in the others, with the most recent additions to the story added.[73] After Schema 276 was definitively edited in late February 1968, it was sent to the consultors. After the suggestions mailed in by the various members were put together, and after a meeting of the members of the Consilium present in Rome in April, the rite was brought to its present state of development by the relator of the study group, Balthasar Fischer.[74] In our study of this schema, only the significant changes will be noted. (This can be followed in detail by reference to the *praenotanda* to the rite, found in part II, section 5, of the United States and Canadian editions of the *Rite of Christian Initiation of Adults.*)

The first paragraph was rewritten and substantially strengthened in this final draft with several additions that hone the text for clarity. The title used to refer to this ritual had been augmented in the early stages of work on the rite. Now this is futher augmented with reference to the Decree on the Eastern Churches, article 4, which speaks of the "fullness of Catholic communion."[75] The reception into the full communion of the Catholic church is qualified by the addition of "in the Latin Rite." The last addition strengthens the text and sets the tone for the use of this *ordo*. Ecumenical sensitivity in the drafting of this text is obvious.

In paragraph 2, also, the text is rewritten and strengthened. The Decree on Eastern Churches 25 is cited, which permits Eastern Christians to make a simple profession of faith without any special ceremony for entrance into the full communion of the Catholic church. Reference to article 4 from the same decree directs that the Holy See is to be consulted in any inter-church disputes.

The next paragraph (5) treats of the doctrinal and spiritual preparation accommodated to the pastoral needs of each individual. There is a change placing more emphasis on the baptism already received, which can be lived more fully in communion with the Catholic church. The paragraph ends with the same warning (however, reworded from the previous schema) to avoid any equating of these candidates with catechumens. Paragraphs 6 to 9 have no substantial changes.

Paragraph 10 deals with the celebration of the eucharist that follows the reception and with those who can receive holy communion under both species. In the previous schema, only the newly received, the spouse (if Catholic), the sponsor(s), the parents and catechists were invited to receive under both species. In Schema 290, this list is extended to all the Catholics who are present.[76] Paragraph 11 is the same, allowing episcopal conferences the capacity to adapt the *ordo* according to the needs of each country and region. An addition to this paragraph is numbered 11bis, which directs that the names of the received be noted in a special register, making note of the day and place of their baptism.[77]

In the outline of the celebration of reception during the Mass, we will only note the changes from the previous schema. In paragraph 12 an addition to the previous schema mentions that the Mass formulary for the Unity of the Church may be used. An addition to the second part of the paragraph describing the elements that should be contained in the homily is also to be noted. Not only is grateful mention to be made of the baptism already received, "but also of the confirmation already received, or to be received, and of the holy eucharist, celebrated now for the first time among his or her Catholic brothers and sisters."[78]

A change in paragraph 14 prescribes the omission of the imposition of hands in the reception if confirmation is to follow.[79] This is significant because it drops what was to be considered the "act of reception." Also to be noted is a change in the formula that is said if the imposition of hands is performed for the act of admission. This change highlights more the role of the Holy Spirit in the life of full communion with the church. The formula begins, "N., the Lord receives you. . . ." The deprecative form has been changed to a declarative form.

Paragraphs 15 and 16 are substantially rewritten. Schema 290 presumes that confirmation will normally happen immediately, although the exceptional case is foreseen in which confirmation will not take place and appropriate directions are given. The text is rewritten and strengthened from the earlier text. The directions for the confirmation are dropped from Schema 290. The rite of confirmation had also been in revision during this time; by the time Schema 290 was written, the form of that revision was known. The friendly greeting with the celebrant taking the hands of the newly received is retained (the substitution of a different gesture is the decision of the local ordinary).

Only one change is made in paragraph 17, which covers the general intercessions. The previous schema directed that the introduction to the prayers should include a mention of baptism and eucharist; confirmation is added to these two sacraments in Schema 290. Paragraph 19 speaks about the offering of holy communion under both species.

The directions for the celebration of reception outside the Mass are exactly the same as those given in the previous schema with one change. A sentence is cut from paragraph 21 that describes the admonition that should be given before the profession of faith.[80] The details of the earlier paragraph (12) are similar to the sentence that was dropped here.[81]

The examples of general intercessions contain two changes from those suggested in the previous schema. Changes in the introduction highlight the action of the Holy Spirit in the sacrament of confirmation and the great joy of the event of admitting a person to full communion in the Catholic church. The other change involves the conclusion if the celebration takes place outside the Mass. An introduction is given to the Lord's Prayer (which concludes the intercessions), with the direction that the concluding doxology to the Lord's Prayer may be added if it was part of the candidate's religious tradition.[82] A final appendix to this schema includes suggestions for scripture readings and the psalm response.[83]

In this schema, a more polished *ordo* and *praenotanda* emerge. Various changes can be attributed to stylistic and linguistic concerns. Other changes clarify the purpose of the rite theologically and liturgically. Some changes are made in the light of a new ecumenical climate (i.e., permitting the use of the doxology of the Lord's Prayer).

During the tenth plenary session of the Consilium, the *ordo* was on the agenda.[84] It was discussed in a special session on Thursday, 25 April 1968, involving the president, some bishop members and study group XXIII-2, as well as Msgr. Arrighi from the Secretariat for Christian Unity. The schema had been approved; however, certain changes were suggested by the members of the Consilium, and these were discussed in this special session and reported in *adnexa ad Schemata* 290.[85]

Three changes were made in the *praenotanda*. In paragraph 9 the members suggested the reintroduction of the qualification of the word "sponsor," so the text will now read, "the sponsor, whether a man or a woman." This seems odd, since in the previous schemata it is not clear that the qualification "man or woman" was ever a part of the text.[86] This change was accepted and appears in the text of the *editio typica*.

The next point answers the question of one of the members (and also one of the observers), "Could the sacramental actions themselves, i.e., confirmation (if it is to be conferred) and especially participation in the eucharistic table, suffice to admit an already baptized person into the fullness which is in the Catholic church?"[87] The subcommission responded to this question citing *Sacrosanctum concilium,* 69b, which called for "a new *ordo* to be drawn up . . . which . . . should indicate that converts to the Catholic faith are now being admitted to communion with the Church."[88] The directives from the

Directory on the Eastern Churches for the admittance to full communion of Eastern separated Christians are then cited. Those directives indicate that only a simple profession of faith is required for them to come into full communion. Nothing similar was said of any others coming for full communion either at the Council or in the First Ecumenical Directory.[89]

Paragraph 5 of this *adnexum* is a change based on the question raised in the above paragraph. In paragraph 19 of the First Ecumenical Directory, the ordinary is granted the privilege of adapting the *ordo* as he sees fit for each individual case. Thus the *ordo* may be shortened or lengthened as the various needs arise.[90] For this reason a change indicating this was made in paragraph 11 of the final text. This change, too, was accepted and exists in the text of the *editio typica*.

Four changes in the actual ritual were discussed. The first change is made for more clarity in the first part of paragraph 12, which gives directions for the Mass to be used. The new text reads, "If the admission takes place on a holy day or Sunday, the Mass of the day is used; if it takes place within the week, even on a feast, the votive Mass for the Unity of the Church (to be newly drawn up) may be used."[91] The earlier text only stated that "even on a feast, the Mass of Christian Unity may be used."[92]

Another change is made in the same paragraph, because it was thought by some that the admonition to the convert was a bit too triumphalistic. Also, the members of the Consilium wished to refer to the person's free choice in deciding to come into the Catholic church.

In paragraph 13 of the previous schema, the members felt that the formula added at the end of the Creed by the candidate was a "little too abstract." For this reason, they suggested the addition of "proclaim," so the new formula reads, "I believe and profess all that the Holy Catholic Church believes, teaches and proclaims to be revealed by God."

The last suggestion dealt with paragraph 25 of Schema 290, which treats the celebration of penance for the candidate when the celebration of reception happens outside the Mass. The paragraph was rewritten to be clearer, but in the final text of the *editio typica* this paragraph is dropped. In addition, the phrase in paragraph 8 allowing participation in a communal reconciliation service with general absolution is also dropped.

Editio Typica

Editio typica is the designation given the official Latin version of the various rites prepared by the Congregation for Divine Worship and the Discipline of the Sacraments, as it is now called. The *editio typica* for the *Ordo Initiationis Christianae Adultorum* (OICA) was promulgated 6 January 1972.[93] The *editio typica* of the Rite of Reception *(Ordo admissionis)* is an appendix in the OICA. In comparing the text of the *editio typica* of the *Ordo admissionis* with the last schema (Schema 290 and *Adnexa ad Schema* 290), we find some changes for reasons of language and style, along with three significant changes.

As mentioned above, the paragraph about the celebration of penance when the Rite of Reception is celebrated outside the Mass was dropped from the *editio typica*. This allowed celebration of penance after the reception. Also, other changes were made in the paragraph on the sacrament of penance, so that it now says,

> If the profession of faith and reception take place within Mass, the candidate, according to his or her own conscience, should make a confession of sins beforehand, first informing the confessor that he or she is about to be received into full communion. Any confessor who is lawfully approved may hear the candidate's confession.[94]

There is no indication of what the practice should be if the profession and reception happens outside the Mass.

Also, note that the sentence offering the possibility of the candidate participating in a communal service with general absolution is dropped.[95]

The text of the *editio typica* also contains an addition that is completely new. Paragraph 7 of the *Ordo admissionis* describes the church's stance on baptism and the prohibition against rebaptism. The text also describes what should be done in case a candidate needs to be conditionally rebaptized.[96] The text also cites numbers 14 and 15 of the First Ecumenical Directory,[97] which state emphatically that the practice of conditional baptism without distinction of all who seek full communion must be stopped. The case is stated strongly, and, no doubt because of pastoral necessity, it was thought necessary to include a mention of this in the *editio typica*. For the rest of the *ordo*, the *editio typica* is the same as that of the last schema.

A final change should be noted in the formula for reception that makes the reception more specific. The text in the *editio typica* reads, "N., the Lord receives you . . . into the Catholic Church."[98] The specification "into the Catholic Church" articulates further that the person is received into the full communion of the Catholic Church.[99]

Summation

This chapter has undertaken the study of the actual formation of the Rite of Reception of Baptized Christians into the Full Communion of the Catholic Church *(Ordo admissionis valide iam baptizatorum in plenam communionem ecclesiae catholicae)*. The chapter began with a brief look at the documents concerned with the beginning of the liturgical reform.

To place the Consilium's work on the *Ordo admissionis* in context, an overview of its work on Christian initiation in general was presented, followed by the analysis of the five schemata and the one *adnexum* concerned with this *ordo.* Each schema was analyzed in detail, and this investigation has uncovered the process of drafting the new *ordo,* along with some of the motivations and rationale for various choices made. Finally, the *editio typica* was presented briefly, with the final changes (different from the final schema) noted.

The final chapter will be a presentation of the Rite of Reception as it appears in the ritual books for use in the Catholic church in the United States of America. This will be followed by an evaluation of the ritual and adaptations based on insights gained from the historical study.

Chapter 6

Adaptation and Evaluation

■

In this chapter the Rite of Reception will be presented and evaluated as it appears in the liturgical books for use in the dioceses of the United States of America. The 1988 edition of the *Rite of Christian Initiation of Adults* for the United States[1] includes all the rites for the Christian initiation of adults, followed by several adaptations. Four optional rites are included under the title Preparation of Uncatechized Adults for Confirmation and Eucharist.[2] These rites are intended for two groups of people: persons who were baptized in the Catholic church and had no catechetical formation (thus were never confirmed or received eucharist), and persons baptized in other Christian communities who had no further catechetical formation.[3] These optional rites are followed in the RCIA by the *Ordo admissionis,* under the title Reception of Baptized Christians into the Full Communion of the Catholic Church.[4] Appendix I follows, consisting of combined rites for use when catechumens are preparing for the sacraments of Christian initiation and when validly baptized (whether in the Catholic church or not) but uncatechized adults are preparing to complete their Christian initiation or preparing to be received into the full communion of the Catholic church. Appendix III contains the National Statutes for the Catechumenate.

This chapter will present, first, the special provisions noted in the National Statutes for the Catechumenate, followed by a more detailed look at the adapted rites.[5] The second part of the chapter will bring this study to completion with an evaluation of the *editio typica* and the adaptations found in the RCIA ritual edition, based on insights from the historical study.

Regulation and Adaptation of the Rite of Reception in the United States

The National Statutes for the Catechumenate

The National Statutes for the Catechumenate were approved by the National Conference of Catholic Bishops on 11 November 1986.[6] These statutes govern use of the *Ordo initiationis christianae adultorum* in the Catholic church in the United States, and give instruction for use of the ritual with catechumens and candidates.[7] The National Statutes make a clear distinction between catechumens and candidates. *Candidate* is the word used to refer to the validly baptized preparing for reception into full communion. *Convert* should be used only for those coming to Christian faith from unbelief.[8]

Eight paragraphs (nos. 30–37) of the National Statutes concern the Rite of Reception directly. Paragraph 30 emphasizes that the validly baptized should not be treated as catechumens. Their preparation needs to be determined "according to the individual case," depending on their background.[9] Paragraph 31 offers some suggestions regarding their formation. Those candidates who have "received relatively little Christian upbringing may participate in the elements of catechumenal formation so far as necessary and appropriate," but should not be equated with the catechumens in any way when celebrating the rites. For these persons, some of the optional rites from the section titled Preparation of Uncatechized Adults for Confirmation and Eucharist may be appropriate. Other candidates, who have "lived as Christians," should not be subjected to a "full program parallel to the catechumenate," but "to a period of instruction in the Catholic tradition and a degree of probation within the Catholic community."[10]

The next three paragraphs in this section speak about the celebration of the ritual. The reception should ordinarily take place at the Sunday eucharist of the community.[11] It "is preferable that reception . . . not take place at the Easter Vigil lest there be any confusion" between the baptized and the elect who will be baptized.[12] However, if the reception is to take place at the Easter Vigil, the combined rite should be used. Care should be taken to maintain the distinction between the validly baptized being received into full communion and the elect who will celebrate sacramental initiation.[13]

Paragraph 35 of the National Statutes indicates that confirmation is to be celebrated whenever the Rite of Reception is celebrated, whether by bishop or delegated presbyter. The *ordo* "respects the traditional sequence of confirmation before eucharist." If a diocesan bishop wishes to confirm those received into full communion, he "should reserve the rite of reception to himself."[14] The following paragraph mentions that the sacrament of reconciliation should be celebrated prior to the reception, distinct from the rite of reception itself. The candidates are to be encouraged to celebrate the sacrament frequently.[15] The final paragraph of the National Statutes gives the restrictions and the form under which conditional baptism should be given. It should only be performed after careful investigation, then, if deemed necessary, done privately, apart from the rite of reception.[16]

Preparation of Baptized, Uncatechized Adults

The National Conference of Catholic Bishops approved the inclusion in the RCIA of several optional rites for "adults who were baptized as infants either as Roman Catholics or as members of another Christian community, but did not receive further catechetical formation nor, consequently, the sacraments of confirmation and eucharist."[17] This study will treat the adaptations from the perspective of use with validly baptized persons coming from other Christian churches; they will not be commented on as they pertain to baptized, uncatechized Catholics. The proposed adaptations are an attempt to meet the needs of the various situations of persons coming to the Catholic church.[18]

The introduction states that although these persons may "have not yet heard the message of the mystery of Christ," they are treated different from catechumens by the fact of their having been baptized. They are already members of the church; "hence, their conversion is based on the baptism they have already received, the effects of which they must develop."[19] It is foreseen that these candidates might follow a program that "corresponds to the one laid down for catechumens . . . [always taking] into account that these adults have a special status because they are already baptized."[20] The entire Christian community is enjoined to help these candidates grow in love and prayer and to testify to their readiness for admittance to the sacraments.[21] A sponsor presents them to the community and journeys with them in the process.[22]

The candidates may take part in liturgical celebrations in their preparation for the reception of the sacraments. The rites discussed in this section are optional. The rites for baptized candidates preparing for the completion of their sacramental initiation or reception into full communion are the Rite of Welcoming the Candidates, the Rite of Sending the Candidates for Recognition by the Bishop and for the Call to Continuing Conversion, the Rite of Calling the Candidates to Continuing Conversion and a Penitential Rite (Scrutiny). These rites were drawn up under the auspices of the Bishops' Committee on the Liturgy of the National Conference of Catholic Bishops and are designed following the model of the catechumenal rites. They appear in appendix I of the U.S. edition of the RCIA.

Rite of Welcoming the Candidates: The purpose of this rite is to introduce to the community and welcome candidates who are preparing

> to complete their Christian initiation through the sacraments of confirmation and/or eucharist or to be received into the full communion of the Catholic church. The prayers and ritual gestures acknowledge that the validly baptized are already part of the community because they have been marked by baptism. Now the church surrounds them with special care and support as they prepare to be sealed with the gift of the Spirit in confirmation and take their place at the banquet table of Christ's sacrifice.[23]

This rite was created following the outline of the Rite of Acceptance into the Order of Catechumens. A brief comparison of the structure will show the similarity between the two rites.

Rite of Welcoming the Candidates	Rite of Acceptance into the Order of Catechumens
Welcoming the Candidates	Receiving the Candidates
Greeting	Greeting
Opening Dialogue	Opening Dialogue
Candidates' Declaration of Intent	Candidates' First Acceptance of the Gospel
Affirmation by the Sponsors and the Assembly	Affirmation by the Sponsors and the Assembly
Signing of the Candidates with the Cross	Signing of the Candidates with the Cross

Signing of the Forehead	Signing of the Forehead
[Signing of the Other Senses]	[Signing of the Other Senses]
Concluding Prayer	Concluding Prayer
	Invitation to the Celebration of the Word of God
Liturgy of the Word	Liturgy of the Word
Instruction	Instruction
Readings	Readings
Homily	Homily
[Presentation of a Bible]	[Presentation of a Bible]
Profession of Faith	
General Intercessions	Intercessions for the Catechumens
Prayer over the Candidates	Prayer over the Catechumens
[Dismissal of the Assembly]	Dismissal of the Catechumens
Liturgy of the Eucharist	Liturgy of the Eucharist

The opening dialogue is followed by either the candidates' declaration of intent or (in the case of catechumens) the candidates' first acceptance of the gospel. The intercessions in the Rite of Acceptance are prayers only for the catechumens; in the Rite of Welcoming the Candidates, general intercessions are prayed because the candidates are already among the baptized. The Rite of Acceptance includes a dismissal of the catechumens after the prayer over the catechumens. The baptized candidates are not dismissed before the liturgy of the eucharist.

If the parish is welcoming both persons for full initiation (baptism, confirmation and eucharist) and persons for reception into full communion, the combined rite is used.[24] All of the elements in the above table are included, with the signing of the senses of the two groups. The only changes are the intercessions and the concluding prayer. The intercessions are "for the catechumens and candidates," and the concluding prayer is a combined prayer over both groups. According to the rubric of this ritual,[25] only the catechumens are dismissed; the candidates remain for the liturgy of the eucharist.

Rite of Sending the Candidates for Recognition by the Bishop and for the Call to Continuing Conversion: This is an optional rite provided for use in the parish church "whose candidates seeking to complete their Christian initiation or to be received into the full communion of the Catholic church will be recognized by the bishop in a subsequent celebration (for example, at the cathedral with the bishop)."[26] It is fitting that the bishop recognize these candidates; he is the sign of unity within the particular church, and it is his "office . . . to receive baptized Christians into the full communion of the Catholic church."[27] The ritual is intended as a public recognition on the part of the community that the candidates and catechumens are prepared to move to the celebration of the sacraments.[28] It is celebrated in the parish church at a suitable time.[29] This rite parallels the catechumenal rite of Sending the Catechumens for Election and is an optional rite in the catechumenate.

Rite of Sending the Candidates for Recognition	Sending of the Catechumens for Election [Optional]
Liturgy of the Word	Liturgy of the Word
Homily	Homily
Presentation of the Candidates	Presentation of the Catechumens
Affirmation by the Sponsors [and the Assembly]	Affirmation by the Godparents [and the Assembly]
General Intercessions	Intercessions for the Catechumens
Prayer over the Candidates [Dismissal of the Assembly]	Prayer over the Catechumens Dismissal
Liturgy of the Eucharist	Liturgy of the Eucharist

In the celebration of the combined rite for candidates and catechumens, it is noted that the community makes the

> preliminary judgment . . . concerning the catechumens' state of formation and progress. . . . [T]hose who . . . are preparing for reception into the full communion of the Catholic church are also included in this rite, since they too will be presented **99**

to the bishop at the celebration of the rite of election for catechumens.[30]

If the combined rite is celebrated, it is done "in the parish church at a suitable time prior to the rite of election."[31] The objective of this particular ritual is recognition by the community of the "progress they have made in their spiritual formation" and to ask for the "blessings and prayers" of the community as they go to the celebration with the bishop.[32]

Rite of Calling the Candidates to Continuing Conversion: The intention of this rite is to recognize those candidates making the spiritual journey to full communion with the Catholic church. This ritual is celebrated at the beginning of Lent in the parish, unless it is combined with the Rite of Election of catechumens in which case it is normally celebrated with the bishop.[33] It is simpler than the parallel catechumenal rite. A comparison of the structure of the two rites will show the parallels:

Rite of Calling the Candidates to Continuing Conversion	Rite of Election or Enrollment of Names
Liturgy of the Word	Liturgy of the Word
Homily	Homily
Presentation of the Candidates for Confirmation and Eucharist	Presentation of the Catechumens
Affirmation by the Sponsors [and the Assembly]	Affirmation by the Godparents [and the Assembly]
	Invitation and Enrollment of Names
Act of Recognition	Act of Admission or Election
General Intercessions	Intercessions for the Elect
Prayer over the Candidates	Prayer over the Elect
[Dismissal of the Assembly]	Dismissal of the Elect
Liturgy of the Eucharist	Liturgy of the Eucharist

"It is the office of the bishop to receive persons into the full communion of the Catholic church."[34] The combined rite is drawn up to help make this connection for the diocesan church. In the celebration, the bishop asks for the testimony of the community concerning the readiness of these candidates to be received into full communion. Questions are put to the sponsors and the community, and the bishop urges the candidates to "hear the Lord's call to conversion and be faithful [to their] baptismal covenant."[35]

Penitential Rite (Scrutiny): This rite "mark[s] the Lenten period of purification" of baptized candidates. It is to be kept separate and distinct from the scrutinies for the elect; thus no combined rite is provided in appendix I. The rite is intended for candidates nearing the celebration of the Rite of Reception; "its celebration presumes that the candidates are approaching the maturity of faith and understanding requisite for fuller life in the community."[36] It may be celebrated on the Second Sunday of Lent or on a Lenten weekday, and may be used to help prepare the candidates for the celebration of the sacrament of penance. If the candidates are to be received into full communion at a time other than Easter, it may be celebrated at "the most suitable time." This rite unfolds as follows:

> Greeting and Introduction
> Prayer
>
> Liturgy of the Word
> > Readings
> > Homily
> > Invitation to Silent Prayer
> > Intercessions for the Candidates
> > Prayer over the Candidates
> > [Dismissal of the Assembly]
>
> Liturgy of the Eucharist

The rite should be introduced in such a way that all the participants (candidates, sponsors, catechists, assembly, priests) "hear the comforting message of pardon of sin, for which they will praise the Father's mercy."[37] After

101

the readings from sacred scripture and the homily, the celebrant addresses

> the assembly of the faithful, inviting them to pray in silence and to ask that the candidates will be given a spirit of repentance, a deepened sense of sin, and the true freedom of the children of God.
>
> The celebrant then addresses the candidates, inviting them also to pray in silence and suggesting that as a sign of their inner spirit of repentance they bow their heads or kneel. [38]

The ritual continues with intercessions for the candidates and two prayers. The first prayer asks that God may open their hearts and minds to the presence of Christ in their lives, and that the candidates may acknowledge their sins and failings. This is followed by an imposition of hands and a prayer for the pouring out of the Holy Spirit on them.[39] This set of prayers is intended for use if the rite is celebrated on the Second Sunday of Lent; the prayers are linked to the Transfiguration gospel, proclaimed on that Sunday. Another set of orations is included for use if the rite is celebrated at other times.

Celebration at the Easter Vigil of the Sacraments of Initiation and of the Rite of Reception into the Full Communion of the Catholic Church: As the title suggests, this is the combined rite for use at the Vigil.[40] The Congregation for Divine Worship and the Discipline of the Sacraments and the Secretariat for Promoting Christian Unity raised serious concerns, both liturgical and ecumenical, when asked to confirm the use of a combined rite for celebration at the Easter Vigil.[41] It was argued that nothing should be added to the rite of baptism and confirmation of the neophytes at the Easter Vigil. Also, it was noted that the Rite of Reception has its own character and suggestions for celebration, and care should be taken not to confuse candidates with catechumens. There was concern that insertion of the Rite of Reception into the Easter Vigil might harm ecumenical relations.[42] The combined rite for use at the Easter Vigil was accepted finally as an "amelioration of an unsatisfactory condition and not a step in an undesirable direction,"[43] because the two rites were being combined unofficially with some questionable results.

The *praenotanda* offer some considerations for use of the combined rite. "Pastoral considerations may suggest" the celebration of reception into full communion, along with the celebration of the sacraments of initiation for the elect.[44] Celebration of reception into full communion at the Easter Vigil "may also be opportune liturgically, especially when the candidates have undergone a lengthy period of spiritual formation coinciding with Lent." The candidates can make the profession of faith by joining the community in the renewal of baptismal promises. If they have not been validly confirmed, they are to be confirmed.

> Since . . . baptism points to complete entrance into eucharistic communion, the baptismal themes of the Easter Vigil can serve to emphasize why the high point of the candidates' reception is their sharing in the eucharist with the Catholic community for the first time.

When the celebration of reception is part of the Easter Vigil, ecumenical sensitivities should be taken into account as well as the personal preferences of those to be received. When the combined rite is used for the Easter Vigil, there should never be anything equating the candidates with the catechumens. The celebration should "reflect the status of candidates for reception . . . [since] such candidates have already been incorporated into Christ in baptism." The liturgy is arranged as follows:

Service of Light
Liturgy of the Word
Celebration of Baptism
    (The rite of baptism for the elect happens here.)
Renewal of Baptismal Promises

Invitation
Renewal of Baptismal Promises
   Renunciation of Sin
   Profession of Faith
   Sprinkling with Baptismal Water
Celebration of Reception
   Invitation
   Profession by the Candidates
   Act of Reception
Celebration of Confirmation
   Invitation
   Laying on of Hands
   Anointing with Chrism
Liturgy of the Eucharist[45]

The celebration of reception is taken from the Rite of Reception. The texts for the invitation, profession by the candidates and act of reception are all taken from the ritual. The celebrant's sign of welcome[46] is omitted from the rite. Confirmation follows as in the ritual for confirmation, except for the invitation, which is modified.[47] No physical imposition of hands is called for in the combined rite for the Easter Vigil. The imposition of hands at the act of reception is omitted if confirmation follows, as would usually be the case. If the candidate is already confirmed, the celebrant is directed to lay his right hand on the person's head.[48] In the laying on of hands in the confirmation rite, the celebrant is directed to "hold his hands outstretched over the entire group of those to be confirmed" while praying the confirmation prayer.[49] For the candidates, "eucharistic communion is the high point of their reception." This may be mentioned before the assembly is invited to receive holy communion.[50]

Summation

The adaptations and statutes drawn up by the Roman Catholic bishops of the United States were presented in the above section. These are proposed following *Sacrosanctum concilium,* 63b, which calls for the drawing up of local rituals adapted linguistically and otherwise to the needs of different regions. These particular rituals need the confirmation of the Apostolic See. The adaptations seek to meet the needs of various situations of persons seeking to be received into full communion.

This study turns now to an evaluation of the Rite of Reception and its adaptation offered in the RCIA.

Evaluation of the *Ordo Admissionis*

Recalling that the council fathers asked for the rites to be simplified as needed and restored to their original vigor (SC, 62, 50), this study concludes with an analysis of the ritual and the adaptations. The *ordo* will be evaluated in light of the historical study of the ritual and the objectives of the liturgical reform called for by the council fathers. Next, the adaptations made by the bishops of the United States will be critiqued. Tentative suggestions will be offered for future consideration of the *ordo* and its pastoral use.

General Comments

The fact that the *ordo* is constructed in such a way that the baptism already received is understood as the basis for admission to full communion is very positive. All vestige of seeing these persons as penitents or in need of repentance has been rejected. Conditional baptism is severely restricted. The abjuration of heresy, which had grown to overshadow the traditional ritual gesture of the imposition of hands, was dropped. The new *ordo* was drawn up in a very positive light. It was recognized at Vatican II that all those baptized into Christ are in communion with Christ, although those baptized outside the Catholic church are in an imperfect communion with the church. This imperfect communion is perfected in the celebration of the reception into full communion. In these aspects one can see that the *ordo* was drawn up for the needs of the present day.

Ecumenical concerns weighed heavy in the shaping of the rite. The Secretariat for Promoting Christian Unity was consulted, and an observer from the World Council of Churches reviewed the *ordo*. The publication of the First Ecumenical Directory had a direct influence on the *ordo,* as is shown also in the *schemata.* The Roman Catholic Church's relationship with the Eastern churches (as presented in the Decree on the Eastern Churches) also influenced the drafting of the *ordo.* The profession of faith with the prescription to use the Nicene-Constantinopolitan Creed is also noteworthy, since this would already be familiar to many candidates. When the celebration of reception takes place outside Mass, the final doxology of the Lord's Prayer (used in many protestant churches) may be added.[51]

The fact that the *ordo* is celebrated at the community's Sunday eucharist is also to be noted. The entire community welcomes the validly baptized person into full communion at its principal eucharist. The new *ordo* also clearly intends that the community have involvement in the action by witnessing the reception and entering into the prayer.[52]

These general comments lead to some more particular comments and critical evaluation of individual elements.

Particular Elements of the Rite of Reception
Imposition of Hands: This study has demonstrated that the reception of the validly baptized into the church generally followed the archetype of initiation. An imposition of hands was given to the heretically (or schismatically) baptized for the invocation of the Holy Spirit. What was lacking in their baptism needed to be

completed (or perfected) with the episcopal imposition of the hand(s).

In the present ritual, we find two possibilities for this traditional imposition of hands. First, if confirmation is not to be conferred immediately (the exceptional case),[53] the right hand is imposed on the candidate by the celebrant as the words for the act of reception are said.[54] If confirmation follows immediately, this imposition of hands is omitted, and "the celebrant lays hands on the candidate and begins the rite of confirmation with the following prayer: All-Powerful God. . . ."[55]

A critical evaluation of this substitution—imposition of hands in the sacrament of confirmation instead of the imposition of hands for the Act of Reception—based on a large part of the tradition would have to recognize this as an anomaly. Indeed, an imposition of hands for those coming from the Novatianists is known as the Roman tradition in the time of Pope Stephen I (third century). Pope Siricius I (fourth century) speaks of an imposition of hands with the prayer for the seven-fold gifts of the Holy Spirit. The medieval Roman sacramentaries and contemporary ecclesiastical witnesses offer a prayer for the seven-fold gifts along with an imposition of hands. The *Romano-Germanic Pontifical* of the tenth century contains this prayer with hand-laying. William Durandus in the thirteenth century draws up a ritual that speaks of the imposition of the hand along with the prayer (with other elements reminiscent of the baptismal ritual). In the West it seems that only the Gallican and Visigothic tradition attest to a chrismation in the reception of the validly baptized. While the tradition indicates a ritual action and prayer similar to confirmation, it is not equated with confirmation.[56]

An important strength of the ritual, however, is the fact that the imposition of hands has been restored. In the ritual used after the Instruction of 20 July 1859, the imposition of hands fell out of use. The ritual in the

Collectio Rituum 1964 for use in the United States did not include an imposition of the hand(s).[57] (An imposition of hands was still part of the rite of reconciliation in the PR 1595; however, that ritual was hardly used in practice.) This reintegration of the imposition of hands in the new *ordo* should be seen positively. However, its omission when confirmation follows immediately seems to lessen the strength of this traditional gesture.

Confirmation: Substituting the traditional imposition of hands for the one that occurs in confirmation brings about an ambiguous meaning (here) for the sacrament of confirmation. In the Rite of Reception, confirmation now becomes (or at least appears to be) the act of reception as well as confirmation; confirmation now equals (or means) reception as well as the invocation of the Holy Spirit with chrismation. Wittingly or unwittingly, the scholars involved in drawing up the new *ordo* combined Roman tradition with Gallican and Visigothic tradition. Instead of clarifying the liturgical action, it has confused it further—at least for the sacrament of confirmation. This anomaly becomes even more striking if the combined rite for the Easter Vigil is used. In that liturgy, then, the sacrament of confirmation means "reception" for the already validly baptized and "post-baptismal anointing with invocation of the Holy Spirit" for the newly baptized.

Including confirmation in the Rite of Reception itself raises questions that have been part of the discussion of the reconciliation of those baptized outside the church since the third century. Cyprian's charge that the pope could accept heretical baptism, while repeating confirmation (received from the heretical minister), should not be lost. Some protestant churches, for example, have a ceremony called *confirmation*.[58] The question of confirmation is settled for Eastern Christians: If they were baptized, they were also confirmed since confirmation/chrismation is given immediately at baptism.[59] The question of confirmation among the protestant churches that have such a ritual was not settled in the discussion after the Council of Trent (Cf. Synod of Rouen 1581), nor has it been settled to this day.[60] To reiterate the problem, when confirmation is celebrated in the Rite of Reception, it takes on the added meaning of reception. The theological integrity of confirmation is compromised by this rite.

Profession of Faith: Another positive element of the ritual is the profession of faith prescribed. The Nicene-Constantinopolitan creed is directed for the reception. This is important from an ecumenical perspective because many of the persons coming to full communion would be familiar with this creed from the church in which they were baptized. Very positive also is the fact that the abjuration of heresy was dropped. The focus of the reception is always to be the baptism already validly received.

Language: From the patristic period up to the eve of Vatican II, the reception of baptized persons was spoken of as the reconciliation of heretics (and/or schismatics). These persons were also called *converts* before Vatican II, and indeed the ritual was titled The Reception of Converts (*Collectio Rituum* 1964). *Sacrosanctum concilium,* 69b initially made reference to a "rite of reception for the new convert already validly baptized." This was changed in the final edition of the text to simply "a rite for the already validly baptized." This was the language adopted in the title of the new *ordo.* These persons are also referred to as *candidati* in the new *ordo.* This term, *candidate,* is used in the English translation of the rite to refer to persons preparing for reception into full communion. This language should be seen as a strength; it is neutral to positive and doesn't hold any of the negativity of the ancient language (e.g., heretic).

In short, the new *ordo* has strengths and weaknesses. The creation of an *ordo* is no easy task. Having studied the liturgical tradition of the Western church in this matter, one can see the variety of liturgical celebrations for the reception of the validly baptized. With these considerations in mind, the study turns now to an evaluation of the adaptation of the ritual carried out by the bishops of the United States.

Adaptation of the *Ordo Admissionis* in the *Rite of Christian Initiation of Adults*

The adaptations made by the bishops of the United States have many positive components. The special rites in the section Preparation of Uncatechized Adults for Confirmation and Eucharist provide public liturgical rites that mark the stages on the journey to full communion for the candidates. These rites should be seen positively for several reasons. Their celebration seeks to involve the entire community (with celebration at the Sunday liturgy) in the process. The adaptations mark the conversion journey of those preparing for full communion, and in some way can be significant in reminding the rest of the community of the need for conversion.[61] The Call to Continuing Conversion for the candidates emphasizes the fact that the bishop is the one to receive candidates into full communion even if this is delegated in most cases to all pastors.

The combined rites (appendix I) were drawn up to be used in parishes where both catechumens and candidates are coming to communion with the church. These rites attempt to strengthen the distinction the Latin text makes between catechumens (never baptized, preparing for the sacraments of initiation) and candidates (validly baptized) coming to full communion. In the introductory notes to each of the combined rites, the warning is given to be attentive that nothing in the rite should equate catechumens and candidates. This is in keeping with the provision in the *praenotanda* of the Rite of Reception (5): "Anything that would equate candidates for reception with those who are catechumens is to be absolutely avoided."[62]

Some inconsistencies come to the light, however, in the combined rites. Very similar ritual actions are done to the catechumens and candidates. The signing of the senses is suggested for both groups. Here, the ritual actions speak louder than the words composed to make clear the distinction between the two groups. In the Rite of Welcoming the Candidates, the candidates are allowed to participate in the general intercessions. In the *schemata,* reference is made to ancient custom by which the newly baptized or guests did not pray with the community and were not greeted by the faithful until after they would have prayed together for the first time.[63] It seems inconsistent to allow the candidates preparing for full reception to participate in the general intercessions while not yet sharing full eucharistic communion. A further question would be if these candidates should remain for the liturgy of the eucharist, or be dismissed with a formula distinct from that for the catechumens.

The combined rite for the Easter Vigil has some inconsistencies. The rite is an arrangement of two parts of the Latin text: the celebration of the sacraments of initiation (OICA, 208–234)[64] and the Rite of Reception (Appendix OICA, OA 14–21)[65] In the combined rite for the Easter Vigil, there is no actual imposition of hands prescribed in the ritual text for the reception into full communion.[66] For the act of reception, the candidates come before the celebrant, who says the ritual words of reception to each one; he does not impose hands if they are to be confirmed. For the laying on of hands in confirmation, he stretches his hands over the entire group to be confirmed (neophytes and newly received). The imposition of hands, which is the traditional gesture for the reception of the validly baptized into full communion, falls out of the rite. The celebrant's sign of welcome is also omitted. These elements missing from the combined rite should be reconsidered.

A further incongruity consists in the ambiguous meaning associated with the sacrament of confirmation, already mentioned. This inconsistency becomes even more evident in the combined rite for the Easter Vigil. The celebration of confirmation at the Easter Vigil signifies reception for the validly baptized and the sealing and completion of baptism for the neophytes.[67] Keeping in mind the hesitation on the part of the Congregation for Divine Worship to confirm the combined rite for the Easter Vigil, one may ask if this incongruity figured in their decision.

Suggestions for Future Development

In light of this study of the Western tradition of reception into the full communion of the Catholic church, I would offer the following points for consideration in a future revision, translation and/or adaptation of the *ordo*.

- The place of the traditional gesture of the imposition of hands and its importance in the rite should be preserved in the way the rite is celebrated. This should especially be reconsidered because the Rite of Reception appears in the combined rite for the Easter Vigil in the RCIA.

- The *ordo* should be celebrated so that it is consistent with the church's theology of confirmation.[68] This will obviously need to be preceded by the development of a clear understanding of the sacrament of confirmation and its effects.

- The implications of including the candidates in the general intercessions, and allowing them to remain in the assembly for the liturgy of the eucharist needs to be considered.

Conclusion

This chapter presented the *Ordo admissionis* adapted for use in the United States of America. The National Statutes for the Catechumenate were presented followed by the adaptations prepared by the National Conference of Catholic Bishops. Part II of the chapter offered an evaluation of the OA and the adaptations based on the insights gained from the historical treatment of the question. Finally, suggestions for future work on the *ordo* were offered. Liturgical reform and renewal is a constant in the church's tradition.

Chapter 7

Conclusion

■

This study is offered with the intention to bring
to light the liturgical history of the reception of the
validly baptized into the full communion of the Catholic
church. The present *Ordo admissionis* is a new ritual, and
the moment seems opportune to undertake an investigation of the *ordo*. Inasmuch as possible, the presentation
entered into the historical investigation without bias
about the new *ordo* or the tradition (even if the author
already had some ideas about both). In the course of the
research, some of these ideas were confirmed by the tradition; others were proven untenable. The study was limited in its approach to the topic in that only the Western
tradition was treated. The oriental tradition was not
treated, although account was taken of some significant
elements from the East.

From this investigation the following conclusions can
be drawn based on the facts presented.

- In the Roman tradition, the imposition of hands with a prayer invoking the Holy Spirit was the ritual gesture for the reconciliation of validly baptized heretics. The traditions of Gaul and Spain have a prayer with an anointing and invocation of the Holy Spirit. Because of the inclusion of an anointing (with chrism) in parts of the Western tradition, some saw the reconciliation/reception as similar to (or equal to) the sacrament of confirmation.

- The late Middle Ages offers the witness of a fully developed *ordo* (by William Durandus) with a profession of faith, abjuration of errors, imposition of hands and prayer for the Holy Spirit. In his pontifical there is no equivocation of the reconciliation/reception with the sacrament of confirmation.

- In the nineteenth century, following the Instruction of 1859 from the Holy Office, the imposition of hands and the invocation of the Holy Spirit disappear from the Rite of Reception as it was adopted for use in the USA.

- The new ecumenical climate which developed during and after the Second Vatican Council called for an *Ordo admissionis* that would be as inoffensive as possible to those seeking to be received into full communion.

- As a result of this new climate the abjuration of heresy was dropped, and the *Ordo admissionis* attempts to take a more positive approach to the reception into full communion (leaving behind the more discouraging abjuration/profession of faith used up until the promulgation of the new rite).

- Any similarities with reconciliation/penance (as in the reconciliation of heretics) were dropped from the new rite.

- The baptism already validly received is considered the basis for reception into full communion, the high point of which is eucharistic communion. Because of this, any equation of these candidates for reception with catechumens was (and is) strictly forbidden.

• The traditional gesture (the imposition of hands) has been restored to the rite, along with the invocation of the Holy Spirit (in the sacrament of confirmation).

This book has attempted to present as complete a picture as possible of the historical situation of the reception of the validly baptized into the full communion of the Catholic church. The study was undertaken with the purpose of looking at the history behind the present *Ordo admissionis*. The intention was to look critically at the present rite, and offer an evaluation of it based on the tradition, as well as suggestions for the future development of the ritual and its celebration. It is hoped that this study will improve the celebration of the Rite of Reception by bringing to consciousness the rationale behind the ritual, thus allowing everyone—celebrant, candidate and community—to enter into the liturgy with that full, active, conscious participation called for in *Sacrosanctum concilium*.

Notes

Introduction

[1] *Ordo admissionis valide iam baptizatorum in plenam communionem ecclesiae catholicae, in the appendix to the Rituale Romanum ex decreto sacrosancti oecumenici concilii vaticani II instauratum auctoritate Pauli PP. VI promulgatum, Ordo initiationis christianae adultorum, editio typica,* Vatican City 1972, 1974 *(reimpressio emendata).* Hereafter, refered to as the *Ordo admissionis* or OA.

[2] H. Heinemann, *Die Rechtliche Stellung der Nichtkatholischen Christen und ihre Wiederversöhnung mit der Kirche, Münchner Theologische Studien,* Munich 1964. J. Goodwine, *The Reception of Converts: Commentary with Historical Notes,* Canon Law Studies, no. 198, Washington, D.C. 1944.

[3] T. Mäder, *"El sentido de la inposición de la mano en el rito reconciliador de los penitentes y herejes en la practica eclesiástica antigua,"* Ciencia y Fe 18 (1962), pp. 297-374; F. de Saint-Palais d'Aussac, *La Réconciliation des hérétiques dans l'Église Latine: Contribution a la théologie de l'initiation Chrétienne,* Paris 1943; P. Galtier, "Absolution ou Confirmation? La Réconciliation des hérétiques," *Recherches de sciences religieuses* 5 (1914), pp. 201-35, 339-94. Both Mäder and Galtier give a "penitential" interpretation to the texts from the patristic period (i.e., the reception/reconciliation of the heretically baptized looks more like penance than initiation). Saint-Palais d'Aussac interprets the data as having more an initiation "feel" than a penitential "feel."

[4] R. Oakham, (ed.), *One at the Table: The Reception of Baptized Christians,* Chicago 1995.

[5] P. J. Kenedy and Sons (publishers), *The Official Catholic Directory, Anno Domini* 1996, New Providence, NJ 1996, p. 2057, offers statistics on the state of the church as of 1 January 1996. The Kenedy directory notes that in 1995, 69, 894 adult baptisms and 92,155 receptions into full communion were reported.

[6] *Sacrosanctum concilium,* 69b; AAS, 56 (1964), p. 118. English Translation, A. Flannery, *Vatican Council II: The Conciliar and Post Conciliar Documents,* Collegeville 1975, p. 22.

[7] AAS, 56 (1964), pp. 114, 118. *Sacrosanctum concilium,* 62.

Chapter 1

[1] S. L. Greenslade, *Schism in the Early Church, (Being the Edward Cadbury Lectures delivered in the University of Birmingham 1949-1950),* New York, p. 112.

[2]J. Döllinger, *Hippolytus and Callistus; or, The Church of Rome in the First Half of the Third Century* (trans. and intro., notes and appendices by A. Plummer of *Hippolytus und Kallistus,* Munich 1853) Edinburgh 1876, p. 176.

[3]Cyprian, Ep. 70, 1. English translation, G. W. Clark, *The letters of Saint Cyprian,* Ancient Christian Writers 47, Paulist: New York, 1989, p. 46. See also M. Bévenot, "Cyprian's Platform in the Rebaptism Controversy," *Heythrop Journal* 19 (1978), p. 123. "What Cyprian had inherited was the declaration of the Council of Agrippinus (c. 220) that baptism given by heretics (or schismatics?) was to be ignored, and that those who came to the church from them were to be baptized like any pagan convert.

"This he had grown up with since his own conversion, and as he saw it as part of the very essence of the church, he considered it as of apostolic origin. The church might not always have so acted, but the truth had been revealed (at Agrippinus's Council?), and if they had been mistaken in the past, they had corrected themselves just as Saul the persecutor had done after the revelation on the way to Damascus (Ep. 73, 13; 23)."

J. P. Burns, "On Rebaptism: Social Organization in the Third Century Church," *Journal of Early Christian Studies,* Winter 1993, p. 277, n. 59, however, notes that Cyprian's preference was to try and hide the fact of this *change* (i.e., the practice of rebaptism) in the African position. Cyprian would have preferred to cover this up, however, Firmilian of Caesarea (in Ep. 75) notes this change in the African position.

[4]Cyprian, Ep. 71, 1.

[5]Cyprian, Ep. 71, 2.

[6]Cyprian, Ep. 74, 1.

[7]J. Ysebaert, *Greek Baptismal Terminology: Its Origins and Early Development,* Nijmegen 1962, pp. 330–31. "Pope Stephen's verdict in the African controversy subsequently illustrates the Roman position that these heretics must be admitted with the *manus impositio in paenitentiam.* There must have been little understanding in Rome of the African controversy on the *manus impositio ad accipiendum spiritum sanctum,* for the post-baptismal rite had remained an anointing with the result that the terms for the imposition of hands to refer to this rite fell into disuse. In the struggle against rebaptism it now becomes customary, however, when referring to the imposition of hands as a reconciliation rite, to use expressions which indicate that the Holy Spirit is conferred by this imposition of hands."

[8]Burns, "On Rebaptism: Social Organization in the Third Century Church," p. 398.

[9]Cyprian, Ep. 75.

[10]English translation, Denziger: *The Sources of Catholic Dogma* (R. Deferrari, trans.), Herder: London 1957. *Concilia Galliae: A. 314–A. 506, Corpus Christianorum Series latina* 148, p. 10.

[11]E. Ferguson, "Attitudes to Schism at the Council of Nicaea," in *Schism, Heresy and Religious Protest* (ed. D. Baker) Cambridge 1972, p. 61, n. 4.

12 *Conciliorum Oecumenicorum Decreta* (Jedin), p. 14. Canon 19. "Concerning the former Paulinists who seek refuge in the catholic church, it is determined that they must be rebaptized unconditionally. Those who in the past have been enrolled among the clergy, if they appear to be blameless and irreproachable, are to be rebaptized and ordained by the bishop of the catholic church. . . ."

13 C. J. Hefele and H. Leclercq, *Histoire des conciles,* 1.2, Paris 1907, pp. 989 ff. Canon 7. "Concerning those who return from heresies—Novatians, Photinians, or Quartodecimans—whether catechumens or faithful in these sects, let them not be received *before having renounced all heresies,* and in particular those they have left. Those among them who are called faithful in these sects may participate in the holy mystery, after having learned the creed of the faith and having been anointed with the holy chrism."

14 Hefele-Leclercq, *Histoire des conciles,* 1.2, p. 1000. Canon 8. "Concerning those who return from the heresy of the Phrygians (Montanists), let them be catechized with the greatest care. They must also be baptized by the bishops or the presbyters of the church. This rule is to be observed even for those pretended clergy of this heresy who are held in the greatest esteem."

15 *Conciliorum Oecumenicorum Decreta,* (Jedin), p. 31. Council of Constantinople, canon 7. "Those who embrace orthodoxy and join the number of those who are being saved from the heretics, we receive in the following regular and customary manner: Arians, Macedonians, Sabbatians, Novatians, those who call themselves Cathars and Aristeri, Quartodecimans or Tetradites, Apollinarians—those we receive when they hand in statements and anathematise every heresy which is not of the same mind as the holy, catholic and apostolic church of God. *They are first sealed or anointed with holy chrism* on the forehead, eyes, nostrils, mouth and ears. As we seal them we say: 'Seal of the gift of the holy Spirit.' But Eunomians, who are baptised in a single immersion, Montanists (called Phrygians here), Sabellians, who teach the identity of Father and Son and make certain other difficulties, and all other sects—since there are many here, not least those who originate in the country of the Galatians—we receive all who wish to leave them and embrace orthodoxy as we do Greeks. On the first day we make Christians of them; on the second catechumens; on the third we exorcise them by breathing three times into their faces and their ears; and thus we catechise them and make them spend time in the church and listen to the scriptures; and then we baptise them."

16 Siricius, Ep. 1,1; PL 13, 1133.

17 Innocent I, Ep. 2, 11; PL 20, 475; Ep. 17, 10; PL, 20, 533.

18 Augustine, Ep. 98, 5; *Tractates on the Gospel of John* 5, 7; 15, 4.

19 Augustine, *De Baptismo* V:XXIII, 33.

20 Innocent I, Ep. 24, 4.

21 J. Macdonald, "Imposition of Hands in the Letters of Innocent I," *Studia Patristica* 2.2 1957, p. 49. "It is certain that hands were laid upon heretics when they were reconciled to the church. But some have interpreted this as the reiteration of confirmation, others have identified it with penance." Macdonald continues, "I believe that the letters of Innocent I clearly show that at least this Pope regarded the *imposition of hands in the reconciliation of heretics as their confirmation.*"

[22]Leo the Great, Ep. 159, VI–VII

[23]Ep. 166 [emphasis added].

[24]Council of Orange I (441), canon 1; Council of Arles II (between 443 and 506), canons 16, 17, 26; Council of Orleans (511), canon 10; Council of Epaon (517), canon 16.

[25]Gregory the Great, Lib. XI, Ep. 52.

[26]Ep. 71, 2.

[27]Cyprian, Ep. 74, 1.

[28]Ysebaert, *Greek Baptismal Terminology,* p. 333. He speaks about the special circumstances of Donatists and Novatian's followers.

[29]Cf. Augustine, *De baptismo* V, XXIII, 33.

[30]F. Saint-Palais d'Aussac, *La Réconciliation des hérétiques dans l'Église Latine: Contribution a la théologie de l'initiation chrétienne, Études de science religieuse II,* Paris 1943, p. 160. He notes that some have found in this phrase an identification of the reconciliation of the heretic with the penitents. Saint-Palais d'Aussac shows conclusively the contrary.

[31]Saint-Palais d'Aussac, *La Réconciliation des hérétiques dans l'Église Latine,* pp. 160–61. Innocent I, Ep.

17, 10, also speaks formally about the difference between those needing baptism and those needing an imposition of hands *ad Spiritum Sanctum.*

[32]Saint-Palais d'Aussac, *La Réconciliation des hérétiques dans l'Église Latine,* p. 43.

[33]Lib. XII, Ep. 7.

[34]An abjuration was required for certain categories of heretics in East and West. For an example of an abjuration from the Orient see *L'Eucologio Barberini Gr. 336,* (eds. S. Parenti and E. Velkovska), Rome 1995, pp. 152–58. This abjuration of heresy from a Byzantine liturgical text is commented on by M. Arranz, *Les Sacrements de l'ancien Euchologe constantinopolitain (2): Ière Partie, Admission dans l'Église des convertis des hérésies ou d'autres religions non-chrétiennes, Orientalia Christiana Periodica* 49 (1983), pp. 42–90.

[35]*De Baptismo* XV.

[36]Cyprian, Ep. 70 *et passim.*

[37]Council of Constantinople (381) canon 7, singles out the Eunomians, Montanists and Sabellians.

[38]Leo I, Ep. 159, 7. Leo wrote that these persons were to be confirmed only with the invocation of the Holy Spirit through the laying on of hands *(sola sanctificatio Spiritus sancti invocanda est and per episcopalem manus impositionem virtutem sancti Spiritus consequatur).* See Fisher, *Confirmation: Then and Now,* p. 135. "[T]heir imperfect baptism was to be perfected by hand-laying and the invocation of the Holy Spirit; so their membership in the Catholic church would be established and sealed (Ep. 159, 7). . . . [I]n the fifth

century, when the words *confirmare* and *confirmatio* first came into use in connection with initiation, confirmation meant not just strengthening but *completing, perfecting, or consumating*. Similarly the episcopal confirmation mentioned in canon 2 of the Council of Orange refers to that part of the initiatory rite which had to be omitted when presbyters baptized in the absence of a bishop: the subsequent confirmation supplied what was lacking, completing what was otherwise a deficient initiation" [emphasis added].

39Gregory of Tours, *Historia Francorum,* Lib. II, 31 *et passim,* Gennadius of Marseilles, *De ecclesiasticis dogmatibus, liber* 21; Ildephonse of Toledo, *De cognitione baptismi,* c. 121; Council of Orange (441), canons 1 and 2, Council of Laodicea (343–381), canon 7; Council of Arles II (443–506), canons 17 and 26; Council of Epaon (517), canon 16.

40Council of Constantinople (381), canon 7, witnesses later oriental practice, indicating an abjuration of heresy, and an anointing with the formula, "seal of the gift of the Holy Spirit."

41Saint-Palais d'Aussac, *La Réconciliation des hérétiques dans l'Église Latine,* pp. 70–78.

42Lib. XI, Ep. 52.

43Saint-Palais d'Aussac, *La Réconciliation des hérétiques dans l'Église Latine,* p. 45. It was necessary for those preparing for baptism in the church to develop a sense of repentance for past sins as a prerequisite for being baptized.

44Ep. 2, 11.

45For the reconciliation of heretics, the imposition of hands is present in the following sources: in papal letters from Stephen I (in Cyprian, Ep. 74, 1 and Eusebius, *Ecclesiastical History* VII, 2–3), Siricius, (Ep. 1, 1 and *Liber Pontificalis*), Innocent I (Ep. 2, 11; Ep. 17, 8 and 10; Ep. 24, 4);Vigilius (Ep. 1, 3); Pelagius I, (Ep. 21); Gregory the Great (Lib XI, Ep. 52). The Councils of Arles (314), canon 1; and Nicaea (325), canon 8 also testify to this practice. Leo the Great (Ep. 159, vi–vii; Ep. 166, 2; Ep. 167, 18) mentions the imposition for the reconciliation of both heretics and apostates, and Cyprian (Ep. 71, 2) will allow this for the true apostate.

46Augustine, *De baptismo* III, XVI, 21.

Chapter 2

1*Liber Sacramentorum Romanae aecclesiae ordinis anni circuli (Sacramentarium Gelasianum,* Vat. Reg. 316 + Paris, Bibliothèque nationale, *codex latinus* 7193, ff. 41–56) (eds. L. Mohlberg, L. Eizenhöfer and P. Siffrin) *Rerum Ecclesiasticarum Documenta, series maior* IV, Rome 1960; hereafter referred to as the *Gelasianum vetus,* and GeV plus the number of the oration in the citations from the Mohlberg text.

2GeV, 683, *Benedictio super eos qui de arriana ad catholicam redeunt unitatem;* GeV, 684, *Item pro eos qui de diversis heresibus veniunt;* GeV, 685–88, *Reconciliatio rebaptizati ab heredicis.*

3Cf. Chapter I, Gregory to the Bishops of Spain a propos reception of the Arians by imposition of hands. Cf. also Pope Stephen I, Council of Nicaea (325), canon 8,

Pope Siricius I (384), Augustine, et al. L. L. Mitchell, *Baptismal Anointing,* Alcuin Club Collection 48, SPCK: London 1966, p. 111, believes that the content of the prayer with its pneumatic focus could lead one to "reasonably assume that [it] was accompanied by the same ceremonies as the consignation, that is, the signing with chrism and imposition of hands." He cites witness of the Gallican councils of Orange (441), and Arles II (fifth century), and Epaon (517), which speak of a blessing with chrismation. F. Quinn, however, does not see this as a necessary conclusion. In his article, "Confirmation Reconsidered," *Worship* 1985, pp. 355–60, he cites evidence from the patristic tradition of "hand-laying" with a pneumatic focus in North Africa, Gaul and Spain without an anointing with chrism. Quinn (in the context of a discussion of confirmation) notes that "handlaying is an essential element of baptism, has a pneumatic note and completes baptism from the point of view of both ritual and meaning." It seems to me that Mitchell confounds Gallican and Roman tradition and does not put enough weight on the fact that the councils he cites are all Gallican councils, and the Gallican mode for reception of heretics was with an anointing. Rome, however, seems to know just an imposition of hands (Cf. Siricius I, Ep. 1, 1 for example).

4Quinn, "Confirmation Reconsidered," p. 360.

5Even if these "anti-Arian" tendencies are not as strong as in the *Missale Gothicum.* See J. Levesque, "The Theology of the Postbaptismal Rites in the Seventh and Eighth Century Gallican Church," *Ephemerides Liturgicae* 95 (1981), pp. 14–15. In a study of the *Missale Gothicum,* he notes its "anti-Arianizing" tendencies, i.e., a strong focus, often repeated mention of the Trinity. He describes this as one of the "anti-Arianist" tendencies of the *Missale Gothicum* orations.

6N.B. The doxology of the second oration in this series is much simpler: *per dominum nostrum Iesum Christum.*

7M. P. Ellebracht, *Remarks on the Vocabulary of the Ancient Orations in the Missale Romanum,* Nijmegen 1966 (second edition), p. 199. The use of this "periphrastic construction" implies the reception of a "free gift" for which one depends entirely on the favor of God, and is used as a literary convention as a mark of respect.

8Ep. 1, 1.

9J. D. C. Fisher, *Confirmation: Then and Now,* Alcuin Club Collection 60, SPCK: London, 1968, pp. 57–60. Cf. M. Metzger, "Les Sacramentaires," in *Typologie des Sources du moyen âge occidental* 70, Turnhout 1994, p. 86. Metzger notes that this is part of the "Roman core" of the sacramentary. Cf. Innocent I, Ep. 24, 4, cited in Chapter I.

10One would expect this change to a penitential tone in the prayer from the patristic texts seen in Chapter I. Vigilius I, for example, speaks of a "penitential" imposition of hands as well as a "Spirit" imposition of hands.

11Saint-Palais d'Aussac, *La Réconciliation des hérétiques dans l'Église*

Latine, p. 8, notes the distinction already made by Cyprian. The lapsed are returning *ad veritatem et matricem,* whereas those baptized in heretical groups are coming *ad nos* (Cf. Cyprian, Ep. 71, 1; CSEL, 3.2, p. 772).

[12]Cf. Augustine, *De Baptismo* I, I.2, CSEL, 51, p. 146, *"Nulli enim Sacramento injuria facienda est."* and *Contra epistularum Parmeniani,* II, XIII.30, CSEL, 51, p. 81, "Neutri sacramento injuria facienda est." Cf. Haring, "The Augustinian Axiom: «Nulli Sacramento Injuria Facienda Est,»" p. 89. Haring cites other medieval authors who took up this concept of Augustine and continued to develop it up to and including Peter Lombard.

[13]*Le Liber Ordinum en usage dans l'eglise wisigothique et mozarabe d'Espagne du cinquième au onzième siècle* (Madrid Bibl. de la Real Accad. de la Historia, codex 56) (ed. M. Férotin), *Monumenta Ecclesiae liturgica* 6, Paris 1904. Hereafter *Liber Ordinum* and in citations MoO plus the column number from the Férotin edition. This was recently reprinted with a supplemental general bibliography of Hispanic liturgy. *Le Liber Ordinum . . . Reimpression de l'edition de 1904 et supplement de bibliographie generale de la liturgie hispanique* (ed. M. Férotin, eds. A. Ward and C. Johnson), *Bibliotheca Ephemerides liturgicae subsidia* 83, Rome 1996. MoO, 100–3.

[14]Mitchell, "Baptismal Anointing," p. 142.

[15]Save for the chrismation, this is reminiscent of Augustine. Cf. Augustine, *De baptismo* V, 33, CSEL, 51, p. 290. *"Manus impositio si non*

adhiberetur ab haeresi venienti, tanquam extra omnem culam esse iudicaretur: propter charitatis autem copulationem, quod est maximum donum Spiritus Sancti, sine quo non valent ad salutem quaecumque alia sancta in homine fuerint, manus haereticis correctis imponitur."

[16]Ellebracht, *Remarks on the Vocabulary of the Ancient Orations in the Missale Romanum,* p. 193. She notes several places in the Mozarabic liturgy where this language is used in relation to the eucharistic prayer.

[17]Cf. DS, 139, *Capitula pseudo-Caelestina seu "Indiculus," "ut legem credendi lex statuat supplicandi."* This text is commonly attributed to Prosper of Aquitaine. (Cf. A. Kavanaugh, *On Liturgical Theology,* New York 1984, p. 3.) The language of the oration in the *Liber Ordinum,* shows one example of the "law of supplication supporting the law of believing."

[18]Cf. MoO, 34.

[19]*Sacramentarium Rivipullense* (ed. A. Olivar), *Monumenta Hispaniae sacra,* Series liturgica 7, Madrid-Barcelona 1964. Hereafter referred to as the *Rivipullense* and Riv plus the number of the oration from the Olivar edition.

[20]Riv, 1422–1429.

[21] *"Deus qui hominem ad imaginem tuam"* (Cf. GeG, 2395).

[22]C. Vogel and R. Elze, *Le Pontifical Romano-Germanique du dixième siècle, Le Texte. I (nn. I–XCVIII), Studi e Testi* 226, Vatican City 1963; *idem, Le Pontifical Romano-Germanique du dixième siècle, Le Texte. II (nn. XCIX–CCLVIII), Studi e Testi* 227, Vatican

City 1963; *idem, Le Pontifical Romano-Germanique du dixième siècle, III. Introduction générale et Tables, Studi e Testi* 269, Vatican City 1972. This is also known as the "Mainz" pontifical (hereafter referred to as PRG-X). In the critical text of Vogel-Elze, *ordines* are found as follows: *Reconciliatio rebaptizati ab hereticis* (PRG-X CXXIV), *Oratio super eos qui morticinum comederunt* (PRG-X CXXV), *Benedictio cum impositione manuum super eos qui de diversis heresibus veniunt* (PRG-X CXXVI), and *Reconciliatio cum impositione manuum redeuntis a paganis* (PRG-X CXXVII).

23M. Andrieu, *Le Pontifical romain au moyen-âge, Tome III: Le Pontifical de Guillaume Durand, Studi e Testi* 88, Vatican City 1940 (reprint 1984) (=PGD).

24Andrieu, *Le Pontifical romain au moyen-âge, Tome III: Le Pontifical de Guillaume Durand,* pp. 316–18, 616–19. Also, P. Batiffol, "Le Pontifical romain. II—Le Pontifical de Guillaume Durand," *Bulletin d'ancienne littérature ecclésiastique,* 1912, p. 295.

25C. Vogel, *Medieval Liturgy: An Introduction to the Sources* (trans. and revised Storey, W. and Rasmussen, N. K. of *Introduction aux sources de l'histoire du culte chrétien au moyen âge,* Spoleto: Centro italiano di studi sull'alto medioevo 1981), Washington, D.C.: The Pastoral Press 1986, pp. 255–56. Two centuries later, under the charge of Pope Innocent VIII, A. Piccolomini and J. Burchard edited what is known as the *Editio Princeps* of the Roman Pontifical published in 1485. This *ordo* was omitted by them; there must have been little or no need for such a ritual as the reconciliation of schismatics, apostates and heretics. "In the letter dedicated to his 'all-seeing Holiness' *(Oculatissima Sanctitas),* the authors explicitly acknowledge that they have faithfully reproduced the Pontifical of William Durandus and have confined themselves to correcting the text from several different MSS. . . . Piccolomini-Burchard were content with suppressing the sections of the Pontifical which had become obsolete (e.g., the expulsion of penitents and their reconciliation on Holy Thursday) . . ." Cf. also M. Dykmans, *Le Pontifical Romain revise au xve siecle, Studi e Testi* 311, Vatican City 1985, pp. 152–56. Dykmans lists all the items found in the pontificals published from 1485 up to 1595 inclusive. The *ordo* under study only reappears in the PR, 1595. The suppression of this *ordo ad reconciliandum* from the Pontifical seems all the more strange since the fifteenth century began with the Council of Constance (1414–1418) which dealt with the problems of Wycliffe and Hus (see DS, 1151–1235).

26Riv, 1422. R. Cabie, *"Le Pontifical de G. Durand l'ancien et les livres liturgiques Langedociens,"* Cahier de Fanjeaux 17, *Collection d'Histoire religieuse du Languedoc au XIIIe et au début du XIVe siècles,* Toulouse, 1982, p. 235, mentions this source. The prayer is taken from the *Rivipullense,* Section CCCXXXII, *Ordo ad reconciliandum apostatam a iudaismo, heresi, vel gentilitate conversum.*

27The *ordo* in the *Rivipullense* takes two prayers from the eighth-century Frankish-Gelasian tradition, Riv, 1426, is inspired by GeG, 2395

(GeA, 2018, GeP, 1445) *oratio super eos qui morticinum commederunt* (and more remotely GeV, 687, *reconciliatio rebaptizati ab heredicis—alia minore aetate*). Riv, 1427 is taken from GeG, 2396 (GeP, 1446), *Reconciliatio redeuntibus a paganis* (and more remotely from GeV, 683, *benedictio super eos qui de Arriana ad Catholicam redeunt unitatem.*

In the *Rivipullense,* this prayer is followed by a prostration of the subject in the church while three psalms are prayed, *Miserere mei deus, Benedixisti domine, De profundis.* These are follwed by the *Kyrie eleison, Pater noster* and *Salvum fac.* (Riv, 1424–25). Riv, 1427 is taken from the eighth-century Frankish-Gelsaian tradition, *Domine deus omnipotens pater domini nostri . . . et consigna vel resigna eum signo crucis in vitam proptiatus aeternam* (Cf. GeG, 2396, GeP, 1446).

[28]Cf. PR-XIII, LIII, 21, p. 517, *Ordo ad cathecuminum faciendum, "Ingredere in sanctam ecclesiam Dei, ut accipias benedictionem celestem a domino <nostro> Iesu Christo."* Cf. also RR 1614, pp. 30–31, Cap. IV, *ordo baptismi adultorum, "N. Ingredere in sanctam Ecclesiam Dei, ut accipias benedictionem caelestem a Domino Iesu Christo et habeas partem cum illo, et Sanctis eius."* The *Rituale Romanum* 1614 is used since it is a representative of the earlier medieval baptismal ritual.

[29]Cf. PR-XIII, LIII, 7, p. 514, *Ordo ad cathecuminum faciendum,* cf. also RR 1614, p. 24 Cap. IV, *ordo baptismi adultorum.* Along with consignation in the initiation rituals, the candidate is exhorted to turn from idols (of whatever kind) and embrace the living God.

[30]Cf. PR-XIII, XLIV, 20, p. 476, *[Ordo qualiter agendum sit in sabbato sancto],* cf. also RR 1614, pp. 31–32, *Cap. IV, ordo baptismi adultorum* (All recite the Apostles' Creed, then the one to be baptized is questioned with the three-fold questions along with a second renunciation of Satan).

[31]J. Catalanus, *Pontificale Romanum in tres partes distributum Clementis VIII. ac Urbani VIII. auctoritate recognitum nunc primum prolegomenis et commentariis illustratum, in quo varii manuscripti Ritus Pontificales non modo sparsim in ipsis Commentariis sed et integri in Appendicibus Titulorum referuntur ac notis illustrantur, 3 volumes,* Paris: Méquignon (nova editio) 1850–52, T. III, p. 275.

[32]Riv, 1428. *"Homo, abrenuntias Sathanae et angelis eius? Et omnibus pompis, operibus et imperiis eius? Abrenuntias aetiam omni secte et pravitati superstitionis gentilitatis, hereticae vel iudaice, inimice fidei sanctae catholicae?"*

[33]Cf. PR-XIII, XLIV, 20, p. 476, *[Ordo qualiter agendum sit in sabbato sancto],* cf. also RR 1614, p. 33 Cap. IV, *ordo baptismi adultorum,* "Vis baptizari?"

[34]For the reconciliation of heretics, the imposition of hands is present in the following sources: in papal letters from Stephen I (in Cyprian, Ep. 74, 1–2; CSEL, 3.2, p. 799, Eusebius, H. E. VII, 2–3, SC, 41, p. 167), Siricius (Ep. 1, 1; PL, 13, 1133, and Liber Pontificalis, T. I, p. 216), Innocent I (Ep. 2, 11; PL, 20, 475, Ep. 17, 8 and 10; PL, 20, 531–33, Ep. 24, 4; PL, 20, 549–51), Vigilius (Ep. 1, 3; PL 69, 18), Pelagius I (Ep.

21, ed. Gasso-Battle, p. 64), Gregory the Great (Lib XI, Ep. 52, CCL, 140, p. 952). The Councils of Arles (314) c. 1, and Nicaea (325) c. 8 also testify to this practice. Leo the Great (Ep. 159, vi–vii; PL, 54, 1138–39; Ep. 166, 2; PL, 54, 1194; Ep. 167, 18; PL, 54, 1209) mentions the imposition for the reconciliation of both heretics and apostates, and Cyprian (Ep. 71, 2; CSEL, 3.2, p. 772) will allow this for the true apostate (those once baptized Catholic, lapsed and now returning to the church).

35Parallels are found in the so-called Roman liturgical books (GeV, 683, 684), the Frankish-Gelasian tradition (GeG, 2394, 2396; GeP, 1444, 1446) and the Spanish source (*Rivipullense*, 1427).

36Riv, 1427, Alia. *Domine deus omnipotens pater domini nostri Iesu Christi, qui dignatus es famulum tuum . . . et consigna vel resigna eum signo crucis in vitam propitiatus aeternam.* In this sacramentary, the prayer is placed before the renunciation of heresy. There is no mention of an imposition of hands with the prayer. The Frankish-Gelasian tradition knows this prayer in two versions (GeG, 2396 and GeP, 1446).

37Riv, 1429, "*Tunc fatiat signum crucis in fronte eius, liniens eum sacro crismate dicens: Et ego confirmo et consigno te signo crucis, in nomine patris et filii et spiritus sancti. Amen.*" From the study of the patristic texts, an anointing would be expected in the "Gallican-Visigothic" environment. This would be further buttressed by the fact that the Visigothic Christian church was largely isolated by the Moorish invasions.

38Cf. Saint-Palais d'Aussac, *La Réconciliation des hérétiques dans l'Église Latine*, p. 14.

39Cf. Gregory the Great, Lib. XII, Ep. 7 (February 602); CCL, 140A, p. 977.

40Saint-Palais d'Aussac, *La Réconciliation des hérétiques dans l'Église Latine*, p. 14. This will be especially striking when looking at the *ordo de neo-conversorum receptione* in the next chapter. Cf. also E. Magnin, "*Abjuration (des hérésies, etc.)*," in *Dictionnaire de droit canonique*, Tome I, Paris: Letouzey et ané 1935, pp. 81–82; and J. Goodwine, *The Reception of Converts: Commentary with Historical Notes*, Canon Law Studies, no. 198, Washington, D.C.: Catholic University of America Press 1944, pp. 117–21, for references to other medieval abjurations.

41Gratian, C. I, q. vii, c. 9 (I Friedberg, pp. 431–432=*Corpus Iuris Canonici, pars prior Decretum Magistri Gratiani* (ed. A. Freidberg), Graz 1955). Dykemans, *Le Pontifical romain*, p. 13. Dykemans notes that this paragraph is the only time that Durandus, the known canonist, quotes from the Decree of Gratian. The Decree of Gratian, compiled around 1140, is the first collection of all universal law for the Catholic church; it comprised approximately 3,900 authoritative texts. It is the basis for the young science of canon law and remained the cornerstone of church law until the 1917 *Code of Canon Law* was promulgated.

42Cf. DS, 690

43A. Michel, "Hérésiarque," in *Dictionnaire de Théologie Catholique*, Tome VI, Paris 1947, p. 2207. Michel offers more detailed information about the church's treatment of heresiarchs. Many of them had to recant their errors before being burned at the stake!

[44]Catalanus, *Pontificale Romanum . . . commentary,* T. III, p. 282 ff. Tertullian, *De praescriptionibus adversus haereticos,* c. 30 (Tertulliani Opera, CCL, 1, p. 213), *"Marcion poenitentiam confessus, cum conditioni datae sibi occurit, ita pacem recepturus, si caeteros quoque quos perditioni erudisset, Ecclesiae restitueret."* Also, Leo the Great, Ep. 28, 6 (PL, 544, 773) (Catalanus lists this as Ep. 10, 6, which is incorrect according to the numeration of PL) to Flavianum, bishop of Constantinople, concerning the Eutychians. *"Si fideliter atque utiliter dolet, et quam recte mota sit Episcopalis auctoritas, vel sero cognoscit, vel si ad satisfactionis plenitudinem, aomnia quae ab eo male sunt sensa, viva voce et praesenti subscriptione damnaverit, non erit reprehensibilis erga correctum quantacumque miseratio: quia Dominus noster verus et bonus pastor, qui animan suam poserit pro ovibus suis (Ioan. X, 11), et qui venit animas hominum salvare, non perdere (Luc IX, 56)."*

[45]MoO, 103. *manus inpositio super eum qui de fide catholica in heresim babtizatus est,* and GeV, 685–88, *Reconciliatio rebaptizati ab heredicis.*

[46]*Contra* T. Mäder, *"El sentido de la imposicion de la mano en el rito reconciliador de los penitentes y herejes en la práctica eclesiástica antigua del Occidente,"* Ciencia y Fe 18 (1962), who sees the gestures associated with penance rather than initiation. A study of the medieval liturgical books makes this thesis untenable.

[47]GeG, 2396; GeP, 1446; PGD, Liber II, IX, 8.

[48]MoO, 103.

[49]Cf. Gregory the Great, Lib. XI, Ep. 52.

[50]PRG-X CXXVI and CXXVII. *Benedictio cum impositione manuum super eos qui de diversis heresibus veniunt, and Reconciliatio cum impositione manuum redeuntis a paganis.*

Chapter 3

[1]The *modern* history indicates the practice following the Council of Trent to the reforms of the Second Vatican Council and following implementation.

[2]DS, 852. Canon 9. *"Si quis dixerit, in tribus sacramentis, baptismo scilicet, confirmatione et ordine, non imprimi characterem in anima, hoc est signum quoddam spirituale et indelibile, unde ea iterari non possunt: an. s."*

DS, 860. Canon 4. *"Si quis dixerit, baptismum, qui etiam datur ab haereticis in nomine Patris et Filii et Spiritus Sancti, cum intentione faciendi quod facit Ecclesia, non esse verum baptismum: an. s."*

Canon 11. *"Si quis dixerit, verum et rite collatum baptismum iterandum esse illi, qui apud infideles fidem Christi negaverit, cum ad paenitentiam convertitur: an. s."*

[3]One would have to ask, however, what was the shape of the *abiuratione haeresis et reconciliatione,* since we know that the *ordo ad reconciliandam apostatam, scismaticum vel hereticum* was not included in the printed pontificals from 1485 up to 1595 inclusive. Cf. Dykemans, *Le*

Pontificale Romain revisé au xve siècle, pp. 152–56.

[4]Saint-Palais d'Aussac, *La Réconciliation des hérétiques dans l'Église Latine,* pp. 27–29. He discusses this Council and its import. This Council is also discussed by T. Mäder, *"El sentido de la imposicion de la mano en el rito reconciliador de los penitentes y herejes en la práctica eclesiástica antigua del Occidente,"* pp. 317–19.

[5]Mansi, T. 34, c. 671–72.

[6]Mansi, T. 34, c. 672. *"Caeremonias baptismi supplendas esse, praecedente in adultis abiuratione haeresis et reconciliatione."*

[7]Saint-Palais d'Aussac, *La Réconciliation des hérétiques dans l'Église Latine,* pp. 27–29.

[8]*Pontificale Romanum, Clementis VIII Pont. Max. iussu restitutum atque editum,* Rome 1595 (available on microfilm from CIPOL — *Centre international de publications oecuméniques des liturgies: Un corpus des liturgies chrétiennes sur microfiches,* Paris) (=PR 1595), part III, p. 543.

[9]PR, 1595, part III, p. 550.

[10]N.B. The two *ordines* for Ash Wednesday and Holy Thursday are not for heretics, schismatics and apostates, but for other categories of serious sinners. The Holy Thursday *ordo* is mentioned in the process of drafting the new *ordo.* By the time the actual *ordo* and *praenotanda* are drawn up, any allusion to this *ordo* for public penance is dropped. F. McManus argued against connecting the reception of converts with the reconciliation of penitents in a letter to B. Fischer (McManus to B. Fischer, letter of 18 August 1967, Archives of the Bishops' Committee on the Liturgy, National Conference of Catholic Bishops, Washington, D.C.).

[11]Vogel, *Medieval Liturgy,* p. 267, note 294.

[12]This would be added in a later appendix. Cf. *Appendix Pontificalis Romani summorum Pontificum jusso editum et a Bendicto XIV. Pont. Max. recognitum et castigatum,* Rome 1848 (=Appendix PR 1595/1848). See P. Batiffol, *Le Pontifical romain. I–La tradition du texte du Pontifical Romain, les éditions imprimées, Bulletin d'ancienne littérature ecclésiastique,* 1912, p. 135. The appendix was a concession, added by Pope Benedict XIV, with the letter *Quam ardenti,* 25 March 1752. *"L'appendice du P. R. auquel Benoît XIV a ajouté la formule de la bénédiction papale, contient autre chose: la description des cérémonies du baptéme quand il est administré par un évêque. . . ."*

[13]PR, 1595, p. 447; cf. PGD, p. 616, where *sacerdos* is also included.

[14]PR, 1595, pp. 648–49; cf. PGD, p. 616. No questions are included, only the indication of an *interogatio de fide.*

[15]PR, 1595, p. 650; cf. PGD, p. 616. The PGD has no mention of the bishop taking the person's hand.

[16]PR, 1595, p. 651; cf. PGD, pp. 617–18. The PGD does not specify which hand is imposed.

[17]PR, 1595, p. 652; cf. PGD, p. 618.

[18]PR, 1595, p. 652–653; cf. PGD, pp. 618–19.

[19]*Rituale Romanum Pauli V Pont. Max iussu editum,* Rome 1614 (available

on microfilm from CIPOL), p. 20. English translation, Weller, P. (ed.), *The Roman Ritual: Complete Edition*, Milwaukee: Bruce 1964 (=RR-Weller 1964), p. 76.

[20]However, as our study will indicate, the ordinary often granted a dispensation of this requirement.

[21]RR 1614/1952, p. 30; cf. RR 1614, p. 24. English translation, RR-Weller 1950, p. 72.

[22]RR 1614/1952, p. 46; cf RR 1614, p. 33. *"Verum si probabiliter dubitetur, an Electus fuerit alias baptizatus, dicat Sacerdos: N., si non es baptizatus, ego te baptizo in nomine Patris, et Filii, et Spiritus Sancti."* (N.B. In the first phrase, the *alias* doesn't seem to belong, however, it is verified in the RR 1614 Latin text.) English translation, RR-Weller 1950, p. 115.

[23]A. Fortescue, and J. B. O'Connell, *The Ceremonies of the Roman Rite Described*, Westminster 1953, p. 389.

[24]RR 1614, p. 34, English translation, RR-Weller 1950, p. 119.

[25]Following canon 4 from the Council of Trent on Baptism, DS, 860. In studying the liturgical texts, however, one should remember that in practice the acceptance of a heretic's baptism was very rare, so while this *ordo* existed, it may not have been used often.

[26]Fortescue and O'Connell, *The Ceremonies*, 1953, p. 389.

[27]A. Fortescue, and J. B. O'Connell, *The Ceremonies of the Roman Rite Described*, Westminster 1962 (12th revised edition), p. 365, dispensation of the ceremonies was the norm in England, and (p. 413) in the United States the dispensation relied more on particular diocesan legislation. (N.B. This edition includes a section by Frederick McManus on particular norms for the Catholic Church in the United States of America.)

[28]Cf. RR 1614, pp. 34-36. N.B. The words about sacramental confession are an addition to the *ordo de baptismi adultorum*.

[29]*Collectio Rituum pro dioecesibus civitatum foederatarum americae septentrionalis*, Milwaukee 1954.

[30]*Rituale Romanum 1614 Pauli V Pont. Max. jussu editum aliorumque pont. cura recognitum atque ad normam codicis juris canonici accommodatum*, Rome: Marietti 1952.

[31]*Collectio Rituum ad instar appendicis ritualis romani in usum cleri archidioecesium ac dioecesium foederatarum americae septentrionalis civitatum*, Washington, D.C., 1961. Included in this ritual book are the *Ordo baptismi unius parvuli, Ordo baptismi plurium parvulorum, Ordo supplendi omissa super infantem baptizatum, Pontificalis ritus pro baptismo parvulorum, Ordo baptismi unius adulti, Ordo baptismi plurium adultorum, Pontificalis ritus pro baptismo adultorum*.

[32]*Collectio Rituum pro dioecesibus civitatum foederatarum americae septentrionalis*, ritual approved by the National Conference of Bishops of the United States of America, New York 1964.

[33]The *Collectio Rituum* 1961 includes the renunciation of false worship, but indicates that it is to be omitted according to a letter from the Sacred Congregation of Rites of 27

November 1959 (Prot. H. 10/59). This letter is published in *Ephemerides Liturgicae,* 74 (1960), pp. 133–34. The change in the baptismal rite is a consequence of the change in the solemn prayers of the faithful on Good Friday dropping the words *perfidi* and *perfidia* in reference to the Jews. This is noted in an explanation which follows the letter.

34 *Ordo baptismi adultorum per gradus catechumenatus dispositus,* AAS, 54 (1962), pp. 310–38. English translation. *The Roman Ritual: Complete Edition* (ed. and trans. P. Weller), Milwaukee 1964, pp. 77–109.

35 *Canon Law Digest,* Vol. II, 1943, pp. 182–84. The new formula to be used by converts was transmitted on 28 March 1942, by the Apostolic Delegate, and was approved to be published in the *Canon Law Digest.*

36 Cf. Riv, 1424–25, *"Tunc prostrato eo in pavimento aecclesiae, dicatur psalmus: Miserere mei deus, Benedixisti domine. De profundis. Kirrieleison. iii. Pater noster. Salvum fac."*

37 *Collectio Rituum* 1964, pp. 158–59.

38 *Collectio Rituum* 1964, p. 159.

39 *Instructio S. Congreg. S. Officii, de neoconversorum receptione.* 20 July 1859, in *Codicis Iuris Canonici Fontes: Volumen IV, Curia Romana,* Vatican 1951. pp. 226–29. (Hereafter referred to as Instruction 1859 or the Instruction.)

40 Ibid; *Acta et Decreta,* Baltimore 1868, pp. 292–93.

41 N.B. Prior to this *Instructio* it was to the Ordinary that the Abjuration of Heresy and Profession of Faith were given. See Magnin, *"Abjuration (des hérésies etc.),"* p. 89.

42 The Holy Office did not issue liturgical rituals, but the similarity of this Instruction and the *Ordo de neoconversus receptione* is striking.

43 J. Goodwine, *The Reception of Converts,* Washington, D.C., 1944, pp. 9–10.

44 *Canon Law Digest* (cited above). Goodwine, *The Reception of Converts,* p. 11 ff. provides a side-by-side comparison and study of the text from the Instruction 1859 and the new text. The new text of the profession of faith is found in The Reception of Converts from the *Collectio Rituum* 1964.

45 *Codicis Iuris Canonici Fontes: Volumen IV, Curia Romana,* p. 380. Also found in *Acta Santa Sedis* 11 (1878/1879), pp. 605–606 and DS, 1848.

46 P. Guilday, *A History of the Councils of Baltimore (1791–1884),* New York, 1932, p. 65. The text of the Council's teaching on baptism is found in *Concilia Provincialia, Baltimori: ab anno 1829 usque ad annum 1849, Joannem Murphy et Socium:* Baltimore 1851, pp. 12–13. Sessio II–die 7 novembris.

47 *Concilium Plenarium Totius Americae Septentrionalis Foederatae,* Baltimore 1853, p. 49. Decree XXIII, 0.

48 *Concilia Provincialia, Baltimori,* p. 57–58. *"Decretum quo prorogatur facultas adultos eadem ac parvulos forma baptizandi."* Signed by J. Ph. Cardinal Fransoni.

49 Guilday, *A History of the Councils of Baltimore,* pp. 256–57.

50 Ibid., p. 187 ff.

[51]The very direct attention to this issue easily leads to the assumption that the issue of rebaptism was a problem. If a decree was written forbidding a practice, the forbidden activity must have been happening with regularity.

[52]*Concilii Plenarii Baltimorensis II, Acta et Decreta,* Baltimore 1868, pp. 130–31, Decree 240.

[53]Goodwine, *The Reception of Converts,* pp. 114–15. "In actual practice many heretical baptisms were questioned or declared outright invalid, because of the flagrant disregard for the essentials of the sacrament. The Sacred Congregation of the Propagation of the Faith warned that inasmuch as many protestants think that the faith of the parents rather than the sacrament of baptism is necessary for salvation, they neglect the necessary elements. . . ." Particular legislation in some parts of France and other countries required the bishop to investigate every case for validity.

[54]*Concilii Plenarii Baltimorensis II,* Decree 241, p. 132.

[55]*Concilii Plenarii Baltimorensis II,* Decree 242, p. 133.

[56]*Acta et Decreta Concilii Plenarii Baltimorensis Tertii. A.D. MDCC-CLXXXIV,* Baltimore 1884. pp. 63–64

[57]Guilday, *A History of the Councils of Baltimore,* p. 224.

[58]Ibid.

[59]*Acta et Decreta Concilii Plenarii Baltimorensis Tertii. A.D. MDCC-CLXXXIV,* Baltimore 1884. pp. 63–64.

[60]Codex Iuris Canonici: Pii X Pontificis *Maximi iussu digestus, Benedicti Papae XV auctoritate promulgatus,* Vatican City 1933 (=CIC 1917). All the Latin texts of the 1917 Code are taken from this edition. English translations (unless otherwise noted) are taken from J. Abbo, and J. Hannan, *The Sacred Canons: A Concise Presentation of the Current Disciplinary Norms of the Church,* St. Louis/London 1957 (revised edition).

[61]CIC 1917, c. 12.

[62]DS, 863, *"Si quis dixerit, baptizatos per baptismum ipsum solius tantum fidei debitores fieri, non autem universae legis Christi servandae: anathema sit."*

[63]CIC, 1917, c. 87. My translation.

[64]Abbo and Hannan, *The Sacred Canons,* Vol. I, pp. 23 ff. and 123 ff.

[65]DS, 865 *Canones de sacramentis in genere.* Can. 9 and DS, 867, 869 *Canones de sacramento baptismi,* Can. 11, 13.

[66]CIC, 1917, c. 732.

[67]Abbo and Hannan, *The Sacred Canons,* Vol. I, p. 745.

[68]CIC, 1917, c. 759.

[69]Abbo and Hamman, *The Sacred Canons,* Vol. I, p. 762, citing O'Kane, *Notes on the Rubrics of the Roman Ritual* (new ed., Dublin: James Duffy and Co., 1938) p. 215, no. 441. "This command is all the more relevant in the light of the recent response of the Holy Office asserting the presumption of the proper intention of the minister in regard to baptism received in the . . . sects [mentioned in the following footnote]." See Goodwine, *The Reception of*

Converts, pp. 25–54. Goodwine gives a detailed presentation on determining the validity of the baptism received in heresy.

[70]AAS, 41 (1949), p. 650. December 28, 1949. A doubt was expressed by the bishops of the United States: *"Utrum, in iudicandis causis matrimonialibus, baptismus in sectis Discipulorum Christi, Presbyterianorum, Congregationalistarum, Baptistarum, Methodistarum collatus, posita necessaria materia et forma, praesumendus sit invalidus ob defectum requisitae in ministro intentionis faciendi quod facit Ecclesia vel quod Christus instituit, an vero praesumendus sit validus, nisi in casu particulari contrarium probetur."* The Holy Office responded: *"Negative ad primam partem; affirmative ad secundum."*

[71]Even if the PR, 1595 retains the gesture, as mentioned in the study of that document above, the ritual was probably not often used.

Chapter 4

[1]Prot. N. I C/59, 18 iunii 1959. Letter of Cardinal Tardini to the bishops and prelates of the world. *Acta et documenta concilio oecumenico vaticano II apparando,* Series I, 4 volumes (15 parts), *Antepraeparatoria,* Vatican City 1960–1961 *(=Acta et documenta: Antepraeparatoria)* vol. II, pars I, pp. x–xi.

[2]*Acta et documenta: Antepraeparatoria,* Appendix vol. II, pars II, pp. 3–189.

[3]Ibid., pp. 8–24, *de baptismo.*

[4]Ibid., p. 10. This observation is made by the bishops of St. Paul/Minneapolis and Los Angeles.

[5]Ibid., pars VI, p. 488. This observation is made by Fulton Sheen, an auxiliary bishop of New York at the time.

[6]Ibid., pars VI, p. 365. This is offered by the Archbishop of Los Angeles, Francis Cardinal McIntyre.

[7]Ibid., pars II, p. 515.

[8]Ibid., pars VI, p. 500.

[9]Ibid., pars VI, p. 316. *"Utrum Catechumenatus iterum restitui non debeat in instruendo acatholicos et neoconversos?"*

[10]J. Jungman, "Constitution on the Sacred Liturgy," in *Commentary on the Documents of Vatican II,* Volume I (ed. H. Vorgrimler), New York 1989, p. 4.

[11]A. Bugnini, *The Reform of the Liturgy: 1948–1975,* Collegeville, 1990, Chapter II. This is also treated by G. Alberigo and J. Komonchak (eds.), *The History of Vatican II, Volume I: Announcing and Preparing Vatican Council II, Toward a New Era in Catholicism,* Maryknoll, NY/Leuven 1995, pp. 206–11, 313–18. M. Paiano, *"Il rinnovamento della liturgia: dei movimenti alla chiesa universale,"* in *Verso il Concilio Vaticano II (1960–1962): Passaggi e problemi della preparazione conciliare* (G. Alberigo and A. Melloni, eds.), Genoa 1993, pp. 86–138.

[12]N.B. At this point in this discussion in the preparatory commission, this paragraph is number 54. In the draft discussed on the floor of the council, it is number 53, and it is numbered 69 in the final text.

[13]*Acta et documenta concilio oecumenico Vaticano II apparando,* Series II, 3 volumes (7 parts), *Praeparatoria,* Vatican

City 1964–1969 (=*Acta et documenta: Praeparatoria*), vol. II, pars III, p. 279. (The text of the schema is given in this volume with various *declarationes* explaining that which needs explanation. Pages 275–316 deal with chapter III of the *schema De sacra liturgia*, dealt with in Session V, 26 *martii*–3 *aprilis* 1962 in the *Quarta Congregatio: 29 Martii 1962*.) The complete text of the *schema, De Sacra Liturgia* is published in *Acta et documenta: Praeparatoria*, vol. III, pars II, pp. 9–68.

[14]With the reform of the liturgy the newly converted would be treated much differently than the reception of children baptized privately in emergency.

[15]*Acta et documenta: Praeparatoria*, vol. II, pars III, p. 294. This issue is raised also in the *declaratio* of paragraph 51. This paragraph calls for the restoration of the catechumenate, and the explanation details that this would include the granting of the faculty to confirm to the priest who baptizes.

[16]Ibid., p. 304. My translation. Number 51 calls for a restoration of the adult catechumenate. The *declaratio* proposes the drawing up of a shorter rite.

[17]This distinction, unclear in that discussion, eludes many today insofar as pastoral practice is concerned in the United States. Many parishes have one education/formation process for those preparing for baptism (catechumens) and for those preparing for full communion with the church. Also, in casual conversation with older parish priests, most admit that conditional rebaptism

was the normal practice in the preconciliar period, even if the Holy Office issued a decree accepting the baptism by a number of protestant churches as valid and acceptable.

[18]*Acta et documenta: Praeparatoria*, vol. II, pars III, p. 308.

[19]H. Schmidt, *La costituzione sulla sacra liturgia: testo-genesi-commento-documentazione*, Herder: Roma 1966, p. 118 ff.

[20]Bugnini, *The Reform of the Liturgy*, Chapter III; also M. Lamberigts, "The Liturgy Debate," in *History of Vatican II*, Volume II, Maryknoll, NY/Leuven 1997, pp. 107–66.

[21]*Sacrosanctum oecumenicum concilium vaticanum secundum: Schemata constitutionum et decretorum de quibus disceptabitur in Concilii sessionibus*, Vatican City 1962, series prima, p. 180.

[22]*Acta Synodalia*, vol. I, pars II, pp. 313–14. Bishop Bekkers offers some general comment on the nature of the sacraments as gifts for the universal church, then specific suggestions are offered suggesting that this chapter be called instead *de ceteris sacramentis* since there is a previous chapter on the eucharist. He also makes suggestions about language— *sacramenta* and *sacramentalia*.

[23]*Acta Synodalia*, vol. I, pars II. This is reminiscent of the idea in Augustine's thought: the baptism may be valid but inefficacious.

[24]*Acta Synodalia*, vol. I, pars II, p. 316.

[25]*Acta Synodalia*, vol. I, pars II, p. 349, *Animadversiones scriptae* 11.

[26]*Acta Synodalia*, vol. I, pars II, pp. 351–52; *Animadversiones scriptae* 13.

[27] *Acta Synodalia,* vol. I, pars II, p. 362, *Animadversiones scriptae* 28.

[28] *Acta Synodalia,* vol. I, pars II, p. 370, *Animadversiones scriptae* 38.

[29] *Acta Synodalia,* vol. I, pars II, p. 373, *Animadversiones scriptae* 43. Art. 53. (pag. 180, ln. 27–31).

[30] *Acta Synodalia,* vol. II, pars II, p. 566.

[31] Ibid, p. 696.

[32] Bugnini, *The Reform of the Liturgy,* p. 37 ff.

[33] Jungman, "Constitution on the Sacred Liturgy," pp. 50–51.

[34] A. Bugnini, and C. Braga (eds.), *The Commentary on the Constitution and on The Instruction on the Sacred Liturgy,* Collegeville 1965, p. 165 ff.

[35] AAS, 57 (1965), 76–85, *Orientalium ecclesiarum* 25. English translation, Tanner, Vol. II, p. 906.

[36] *New Revised Standard Version,* New York 1989.

[37] AAS, 57 (1965), p. 19. *Lumen Gentium* 15. English translation, Tanner, Vol. II, pp. 860–61.

[38] Recall Cyprian's position that outside the church there is no salvation. The position adopted at Vatican II puts aside this position

[39] AAS, 57 (1965), p. 93, *Unitatis redintegratio* 3. English translation, Tanner, Vol. II, p. 910.

[40] AAS, 57(1965), p. 95, *Unitatis redintegratio* 4. English translation, Tanner, Vol. II, p. 911.

[41] AAS, 57(1965), pp. 105–6, *Unitatis redintegratio* 22. English translation, Tanner, Vol. II, p. 919.

[42] As the study of the tradition shows, baptism is considered the foundation on which those validly baptized in other Christian churches are admitted into the full communion of the Catholic church.

[43] AAS, 59 (1967), pp. 574–92, *Ad totam ecclesiam* 12. English translation, *Documents on the Liturgy (1963– 1979): Conciliar, Papal and Curial Texts* (ed. and trans. T. O'Brien), Collegeville 1982 (=DOL) 147, p. 320.

[44] AAS, 59 (1967), pp. 574–92, *Ad totam ecclesiam* 14. English translation, DOL, 147, p. 320.

[45] AAS, 59 (1967), pp. 574–92, *Ad totam ecclesiam* 19. (The canon that is mentioned is obviously from the CIC, 1917.) English translation, DOL, 147, p. 321.

[46] AAS, 59 (1967), pp. 574–92, *Ad totam ecclesiam* 20. English translation, DOL, 147, p. 321.

Chapter 5

[1] Bugnini, *The Reform of the Liturgy,* p. 49 ff. He notes that a commission was established by the *motu proprio,* but not given a name. This came later under the suggestion of Archbishop Felici, secretary of the Council. The commission was given the name *Consilium ad exsequendam constitutionem de sacra Liturgia.*

[2] AAS, 56 (1964), pp. 877–900. Discussed in Bugnini, *The Reform of the Liturgy,* Chapter 54.

[3] AAS, 56 (1964), p. 877.

[4] Bugnini, *The Reform of the Liturgy,* p. 579. The members of study group

XXII *(De sacramentis)* were *Relator,* Balthasar Fischer; *Secretarius* Xavier Seumois; and consultors: Frederick McManus, Aemilius Lengeling, Ignatius Oñatibia, Boniface Luykx, Aloysius Stenzel, Joseph Lécuyer, Jean Baptiste Molin. In 1967 Louis Ligier joined as an additional secretary, and Jacques Cellier as a member.

Study group XXIII *(De Sacramentalibus)* comprised *Relator* Pierre-Marie Gy; *Secretarius* S. Mazzarello; and consultors J. Rabau, J. Mejia, Johannes Hofinger, F.Vandenbroucke, D. Sicard. Subsequently added were A. Chavasse, B. Löwenberg, and Corbinian Ritzer.

[5]B. Fischer and P.-M. Gy, Letter *omnibus Consultoribus Coetuum a studiis 22 et 23, 21 julii 1964, Coloniae* (27 pages), Archives of the International Commission on English in the Liturgy, Washington, D.C., summarized in *"Labores Coetuum a Studiis: De recognitione Ritualis Romani,"* Notitiae 2 (1966), pp. 220–30. Cf. Bugnini, *The Reform of the Liturgy,* p. 580–81.

[6]Fischer and Gy, Letter *omnibus Consultoribus,* 21 July 1964.

[7]Fischer and Gy, Letter to the consultors, 23 August 1964, *"Comment envisager le Baptême sous condition (si nécessaire) des catéchumènes venant des Eglises séparées de Rome?"* The term *Églises séparées* no doubt follows language used by Pope Paul VI in his *Encyclica, Ecclesiam suam* (6 August 1964), AAS, 56 (1964), pp. 609–59. Paul VI uses the phrase, *"multi fratres ab Apostolicae Sedis communione"* ("many of our separated brothers"). This language will change again. Cf. John Paul II, *Ut unum sint* will use

"ad ceteros . . . christianos" to designate the validly baptized. Cf. AAS, 77 (1995), p. 17.

[8]Indeed, above in Chapter IV, we saw *Ad totam ecclesiam* 14 and 15, which strictly speaks against the practice of conditional baptism unless there is really a reasonable doubt.

[9]Schemata 236, *de rituali,* n. 22, 11 iulii 1967, *Consilium ad exsequendam constitutionem de Sacra Liturgia,* in archives of The International Commission on English in the Liturgy, Washington, D.C., 12 pages.

[10]AAS, 59 (1967), pp. 574–92. English translation, DOL, 147, pp. 319–29.

[11]Schema 236. N.B. The structure is no doubt the structure that Fred McManus sent to the Bishops' Committee on the Liturgy, National Conference of Catholic Bishops (USA) on 11 July 1967 for their comments.

[12]McManus would have a strong reaction to this in his letter to Fischer, 18 August 1967.

[13]Schema 236.

[14]Schema 236.

[15]F. McManus, Letter to Father Hotchkin with attached proposal, 1 August 1967, Archives of the Bishops' Committee on the Liturgy, National Conference of Catholic Bishops, (USA) Washington, D.C. Attached to this letter is the *principia generalia* and *prima delineamenta ritus* from "one of the subcommittees of the Postconciliar Liturgical Commission in discussion with the Secretariat for Christian Unity."

McManus expresses disappointment in the contents of this proposal, and mentions specifically that he does not want to be "influenced by elements like the imposition of hands to forgive sins."

[16]McManus, Letter to Hotchkin with attached, 1 August 1967.

[17]F. McManus, Letter to B. Fischer, 18 August 1967. Archives of the Bishops' Committee on the Liturgy, National Conference of Catholic Bishops, (USA) Washington, D.C. The quotations in this section are all taken from this letter, unless otherwise noted.

[18]F. McManus, memorandum to Bishops' Committee on the Liturgy, Subcommittee on Liturgical Adaptation with attached First Draft of suggestions, 11 July 1967, in the archives of the Bishops' Committee on the Liturgy, National Conference of Catholic Bishops, (USA) Washington, D.C.

[19]Bishop Bernard Flanagan, letter to Frederick McManus, 13 July 1967, Archives of the Bishops' Committee on the Liturgy, National Conference of Catholic Bishops, Washington, D.C.

[20]Bishop John Morkovsky, letter to Rev. Frederick McManus, 7 August 1967, Archives of the Bishops' Committee on the Liturgy, National Conference of Catholic Bishops, Washington, D.C. #6 of the proposal states: "The individual should be fully instructed concerning the Catholic teaching and discipline of the sacrament of penance, but the occasion for confession should be left entirely up to the discretion of the person."

[21]Bishop James Malone, letter to Rev. Frederick McManus, 11 August 1967, Archives of the Bishops' Committee on the Liturgy, National Conference of Catholic Bishops, Washington, D.C.

[22]Schema 252, *de rituali,* n. 24, 3 November 1967, *Consilium ad exsequendam constitutionem de Sacra Liturgia,* in archives of The International Commission on English in the Liturgy, Washington, D.C.

[23]Schema 252, in the introductory paragraph, this change of terminology takes place and is noted in a footnote. This footnote is carried through the rest of the schemata.

[24]ATE, 19, *"sed professione fidei facta, secundum normas ab Ordinario loci statutas, in plenam communionem Ecclesiae catholicae admittantur."* Cf. Letter, Secretariat for Christian Unity, 17 October 1967, Prot.n. 4565/67.

[25]Schema 252/1.

[26]Schema 252/5. Taken directly from *Ad totam Ecclesiam,* 19, 20.

[27]Schema 252/6.

[28]Schema 252/8.

[29]Schema 252/13. A footnote in the text refers to a letter of Innocent I. Innocentius I, Ep. II ad Victricium (PL, 20, 475B): ". . . ut venientes a Novatianis . . . per manus tantum impositionem suscipiantur, quasi quamvis ab haereticis tamen in Christi nomine sunt baptizati."

[30]Schema 252/13. A footnote in the text refers to the Apostolic Tradition of Hippolytus, XXI (*La Tradition*

Apostolique, LQF, 39, p. 34, *"Et consignans in frontem offerat osculum et dicat: Dominus tecum. Et ille qui signatus est dicat: Et cum spiritu tuo."*) and Cyprian, Epistle 69, 4 (CSEL, 3/2, 719). *"Ex antiquissimis temporibus admissus in Ecclesiam post confirmationem ab episcopo osculo salutatur."* Furthermore, reference is made to an article by Fr. J. Dölger, Der Kus im Tauf und Firmungsritual nach Cyprian von Karthago und Hippolyt von Rom: Antike und Christentum 1 (1929) 186–196.

31Schema 252/13. My translation.

32Schema 252/14. My translation.

33Schema 252/16. A footnote in the text refers again to Hippolytus, Apostolic Tradition XXI *"Antiquissimus mos est quod fideles adstantes neoconfirmatum non salutant nisi postquam prima vice cum eo oraverint; osculum consideratur tamquam 'signaculum orationis'."* (Cf. *La Tradition Apostolique, LQF,* 39, p. 54, *"Et postea iam simul cum omni populo orent, non promum orantes cum fidelibus nis omnia haec fuerint consecuti. Et cum oraverint, de ore pacem offerant."*)

34Schema 252/18. My translation.

35Schemata 256, *de rituali,* n. 25, 20 November 1967 *Consilium ad exsequendam constitutionem de Sacra Liturgia,* in archives of The International Commission on English in the Liturgy, Washington, D.C.

36Schema 256. His name is mentioned in the introductory paragraph. Bugnini, *The Reform of the Liturgy,* p. 595, lists his name as Feiner.

37Schemata for Session IX of the Consilium, November 1967: Notes of F. McManus found in the archives of the International Commission on English in the Liturgy, Washington, D.C. Notes prepared for the November 1967 meeting of the Consilium. Commenting on the issue of confirming adults in the confirmation schema (Schema 240), McManus writes, "The permission to confirm adults . . . is very important. If the adult who is baptized (or the adult who is received into full communion with the church) is not confirmed on the occasion of his baptism (or reception), he should not be admitted to the eucharist. This creates an anomalous situation and suggests that—while it is most desirable for the Bishop to take part in the baptism of adults and in the reception of those already baptized into communion—the priest who in fact officiates should be permitted to administer confirmation before the eucharistic liturgy."

38Schemata for Session IX of the Consilium, November 1967, Notes of F. McManus.

39Schema 256/18.

40Schema 276, *de rituali,* n. 26, 8 March 1968, *Consilium ad exsequendam constitutionem de Sacra Liturgia,* in archives of The International Commission on English in the Liturgy, Washington, D.C.

41Meeting reported in *Notitiae* 3 (1967) p. 477. The meeting took place from 26 to 30 December 1967.

42Schema 276 Bugnini, *The Reform of the Liturgy,* p. 595, notes this information too, however in his account, the places where the work was done are jumbled.

43Schema 276/2.

44Schema 276/3.

45Schema 276/4.

46Schema 276/5.

47Schema 276/5.

48English translation from "Reception of Baptized Christians into the Full Communion of the Catholic Church," in *Rite of Christian Initiation of Adults,* ICEL: Washington, D.C., 1985, p. 226.

49Schema 276/7.

50Schema 276/7. *"Uti generaliter propositum et a Patribus 'Consilii' acceptatum est mense novembri 1967 in schemata 240, De Pont. 16: De Confirmatione n. 15."*

51Schema 256/6.

52Schema 276/8.

53*Ad totam Ecclesiam* 19, AAS, 59 (1967), pp. 574–92.

54Schema 276/12.

55Schema 276/13. There are two footnotes in the text. One describes the manner in which this is to be done if this celebration is part of the Easter Vigil (i.e., the candidate along with the faithful renew their baptismal promises and *Credo et profiteor . . .* is added at the end by the candidate). The other footnote refers to the words added by the candidate. The Secretariat for Christian Unity (17 October 1967, prot. 4565/67) asked for nothing more than these words.

56Schema 276/14. A footnote in the text recalls the ancient practice in the *Pontificale Romanum, Pars III*

pro reconciliatione, and the letter of Innocent I in a Letter to Victricium (PL, 20, 475B): *"ut venientes a Novatianis . . . per manus tantum impositionem suscipiantur, quasi quamvis ab haereticis tamen in Christi nomine sunt baptizati."*

57Schema 276/14. A footnote in the text tells that this was taken from the Syrian Jacobites. Also, the deprecative form has been chosen. Cf. Denziger, *Ritus Orientalium: Coptorum, Syrorum et Armenorum, in administrandis sacramentis,* Wurzburg 1863, p. 466.

58Schema 276/15.

59Schema 276/16. In a footnote, reference is made to the schema that is concerned with the reform of the sacrament of confirmation (Schema 240/31).

60Schema 276/17. "The general intercessions, which can be prepared by the episcopal conferences, follow the reception (and confirmation). In the introduction, the celebrant should mention baptism, confirmation, and the Eucharist, and express gratitude to God. The one received into full communion is mentioned in the first of the intercessions."

61Schema 276/18. Footnote 12 of this paragraph recalls the ancient practice of the church.

62Schema 276/18.

63Schema 276/19.

64Schema 276/20–21.

65Schema 276/21.

66Schema 276/22–23.

67Schema 276/24.

[68]Schema 276/25.

[69]Schema 276/26.

[70]Schema 276. *Specimen orationis communis,* note 14. This prayer is from the *deprecationem* of Saint Gelasius, pope (d. 496).

[71]Schema 276. *Specimen orationis communis,* note 15. This prayer is from the general intercessions of Good Friday.

[72] *"Decima Sessio Plenaria «Consilii»," Notitae* 4 (1968), pp. 180–84. This session met from 23 to 30 April 1968.

[73]Schemata 290, *de rituali, n. 28, 21 aprilis 1968, Consilium ad exsequendam constitutionem de Sacra Liturgia,* in archives of The International Commission on English in the Liturgy, Washington, D.C.

[74]Schema 290.

[75]Schema 290/1, footnote 1.

[76]Schema 290/10.

[77]Schema 290/11bis.

[78]Schema 290/12b.

[79]Schema 290/14. A footnote in the schema notes that this is inspired by a formula taken from the Syrian Jacobites (cited above in footnote 96).

[80]Schema 276/21.

[81]Cf. Schema 290/12. ". . . *post homiliam in qua gratiarum actione mentio fiat baptismi tamquam fundamenti admissionis, confirmationis recipiendae vel receptae, necnon SS. Eucharistiae prima vice cum catholicis celebrandae."* The admonition *"Magno cum gaudio te nunc invito . . ."* follows.

[82]Schema 290.

[83]Schema 290. N. Emsley, *Christus Lux—Christiani illuminati:* A Study of the Language of Light and Enlightenment in the *«Ordo initiationis christianae adultorum».* Towards a Liturgical Theology and a Liturgical Spirituality, Doctoral Dissertation, Sant'Anselmo, Rome 1997, pp. 95–102, treats the lectionary and general intercessions of the *ordo admissionis* in some detail.

[84] *"Decima sessio plenaria «Consilii»,"* pp. 180–84. This brief report of the tenth plenary session of the Consilium, which took place from 23 to 30 April 1968, shows on the agenda the discussion *de admissione in plenam communionem Ecclesiae.* Also noted is the presence of representatives from the World Council of Churches.

[85] *Adnexa ad Schemata 290: de rituali, n. 28, 29 aprilis 1968, Consilium ad exsequendam constitutionem de Sacra Liturgia,* in archives of The International Commission on English in the Liturgy, Washington, D.C.

[86]Schema 252/9: *"sponsor, persona nempe, quae in adducendo";* Schema 256/9: *"sponsor, persona nempe, quae in adducendo";* Schema 276/9: *"sponsor, scil. persona, quae in adducendo";* Schema 290/9: *"sponsor, qui in adducendo"; Adnexa ad Schema 290/3: "sponsor, nempe vir et mulier."*

[87]Adnexa ad Schema 290/4.

[88]Adnexa ad Schema 290/4.

[89]Adnexa ad Schema 290/4.

[90]Schema 290/5.

[91]Adnexa ad Schema 290/6.

[92]Schema 290/12.

[93]An English translation, the *Rite of Christian Initiation of Adults*, was prepared by The International Commission on English in the Liturgy, Washington, D.C., in 1974. This text was published in 1976 by the National Conference of Catholic Bishops for use in the United States.

[94]OA, 9.

[95]No documents are available to bring further detail to this point of the discussion.

[96]OA, 7.

[97]AAS, (59)1967, p. 580.

[98]OA, 16.

[99]In subsequent documents, no change or legislation is given concerning the Rite of Reception. The *Code of Canon Law* published in 1983 has not been ignored. It does not speak of the ritual of reception into full communion itself. Four canons (11, 1086§1, 1117, 1124) make reference to the code in how it affects those baptized in the Catholic church or who have been received (Cf. canon 11).

Chapter 6

[1]The 1987 Canadian edition of the RCIA similarly includes the translation of the rites of the *editio typica* and adaptations. Because there are differences between the United States and Canadian editions, however, this study will focus on the 1988 U.S. edition. References to the RCIA are to this edition.

[2]RCIA, nn. 400–72. These optional rites are found in Part II: Rites for Particular Circumstances, Preparation of Uncatechized Adults for Confirmation and Eucharist. These adaptations were drawn up under the auspices of the Bishops' Committee on the Liturgy, National Conference of Catholic Bishops (USA).

[3]RCIA, n. 400.

[4]RCIA, nn. 473–501. This is a direct translation from the *editio typica*.

[5]The Reception of Baptized Christians into the Full Communion of the Catholic Church is a translation of the *editio typica* of the OA, thus, will not be presented in detail here as this was thoroughly treated in the previous chapter.

[6]RCIA, appendix III

[7]J. Huels, *The Catechumenate and the Law*, Chicago 1994, pp. 1–2. The National Statutes "have the force of law for all dioceses in the United States of America, superseding any other contrary laws, including universal laws that may be contrary to them."

[8]RCIA, National Statutes, nn. 2, 3.

[9]RCIA, National Statutes, n. 30.

[10]RCIA, National Statutes, n. 31.

[11]RCIA, National Statutes, n. 32.

[12]RCIA, National Statutes, n. 33.

[13]RCIA, National Statutes, n. 34.

[14]RCIA, National Statutes, n. 35.

[15]RCIA, National Statutes, n. 36.

[16]RCIA, National Statutes, n. 37.

[17]RCIA, n. 400.

[18]I.e., some persons coming asking to be received into full communion lived active, faith-filled lives in the

church or ecclesial community in which they were baptized; others were baptized and had little or no Christian upbringing. This is undertaken perhaps in response to the concern expressed in Schema 236, that the fact be taken into account that people come from different situations as expressed above.

[19]RCIA, n. 400. Reminiscent of St. Augustine's distinction between sacramental validity and efficacy.

[20]RCIA, nn. 401–2. ". . . the preparation of these adults requires a considerable time [. . .] during which the faith infused in baptism must grow in them and take deep root through the pastoral formation they receive. A program of training, catechesis suited to their needs, contact with the community of the faithful, and participation in certain liturgical rites are needed in order to strengthen them in the Christian life."

[21]RCIA, n. 403.

[22]RCIA, n. 404.

[23]RCIA, nn. 411–12.

[24]RCIA, appendix I, Rite I, "Celebration of the Rite of Acceptance into the Order of Catechumens and of the Rite of Welcoming Baptized but Uncatechized Adults who are Preparing for Confirmation and/or Eucharist or Reception into the Full Communion of the Catholic Church." This rite was drawn up under the auspices of the Bishops' Committee on the Liturgy, National Conference of Catholic Bishops (USA).

[25]RCIA, n. 528.

[26]RCIA, n. 434.

[27]RCIA, n. 435.

[28]I.e., confirmation and eucharist for those to be received into full communion; baptism, confirmation and eucharist for the catechumens.

[29]RCIA, n. 436.

[30]RCIA, nn. 531–32. The combined rite is titled "Parish Celebration for Sending Catechumens for Election and Candidates for Recognition by the Bishop [Optional]." This rite was drawn up under the auspices of the Bishops' Committee on the Liturgy, National Conference of Catholic Bishops (USA).

[31]RCIA, n. 533.

[32]RCIA, n. 439, citation of the "Presentation of the Candidates."

[33]RCIA, nn. 446–49.

[34]N.B. There is no mention of the *Ordo admissionis* made in the *Caeremoniale episcoporum, ex decreto Sacrosancti Oecumenici Concilii Vaticani II instauratum auctoritate Ioannis Paulis II promulgatum, editio typica,* Vatican City 1984.

[35]RCIA, n. 454. From the Rite of Calling the Candidates to Continuing Conversion.

[36]RCIA, n. 460.

[37]RCIA, n. 464. From the introductory notes of the Penitential Rite (Scrutiny).

[38]RCIA, n. 468. This rite is meant to be kept distinct from the scrutinies for the elect. It is clear that the scrutinies influenced the creation of this rite for the baptized candidates. The scrutinies are "to uncover, then

heal all that is weak, defective, or sinful in the hearts of the elect; to bring out, then strengthen all that is upright, strong, and good. For the scrutinies are celebrated in order to deliver the elect from the power of sin and Satan, to protect them against temptation, and to give them strength in Christ, who is the way, the truth, and the life. These rites, therefore, should complete the conversion of the elect and deepen their resolve to hold fast to Christ and to carry out their decision to love God above all."

39RCIA, n. 470.

40This rite was drawn up by The International Commission on English in the Liturgy (ICEL), Washington, D.C.

41Correspondence found in the Archives of the Bishops' Committee on the Liturgy, National Conference of Catholic Bishops (USA) gives an idea of the concerns raised. Letters from the Secretary of the Congregation for Divine Worship and the Discipline of the Sacraments, to Bishop Malone, President of the National Conference of Catholic Bishops; and Bishop Doyle, President of the National Liturgical Commission of the Canadian Bishops' Conference indicate the tension. (Unless otherwise noted, all of the letters in the following footnotes can be found in the archives of the Bishops' Committee on the Liturgy, NCCB, Washington, D.C.)

42Letter of Virgil Noe, Secretary CDW to Bishop Malone, 18 October 1986, CDW prot. 898/86, indicates that the congregation was unable to grant confirmation for

inclusion of the combined rite at the Easter Vigil in the USA ritual edition. Virgil Noe, Secretary CDW to Bishop Doyle, 1 September 1986, CDW prot. 432/86, indicates the reasons.

"1. Apart from liturgical reasons, an ecumenical motive for not accepting the innovation was given in a letter to this Dicastery from the Secretariat for Promoting Christian Unity: 'The insertion of this rite into the Easter Vigil gives such importance to the event that it may cause surprise and even pain to our fellow Christians and give rise to new difficulties.'

2. The following liturgical reasons cannot be ignored since the Easter Vigil has its own proper character:

i. It is not opportune to introduce new elements into the rite of [b]aptism and [c]onfirmation. Care must be taken to distinguish between catechumens and converts.

ii. The *Ordo Initiationis Christianae Adultorum* provides a proper rite in which the following points are to be noted:

a. the Mass for Christian Unity can be celebrated;

b. the recitation of the Nicene-Constantinopolitan Creed is prescribed as part of the rite of reception (n. 15);

c. the rite of admission should immediately follow the homily.

iii. The third paragraph of the *Praenotanda* states that 'any appearance of triumphalism should be carefully avoided . . . . Often it will be preferable to celebrate the Mass with only a few relatives and friends.' It follows then that there can be no change in our decision of

20 June 1986 [Cf. Letter of Virgil Noe, Secretary CDW, to John Page, Executive Secretary of ICEL, 20 June 1986, CDW Prot. 735/86, in the archives of The International Commission on English in the Liturgy, Washington, D.C.], which stated that the rite of reception into the full communion of the Catholic church could not be celebrated during the Easter Vigil." A final paragraph expresses the regret of the CDW to learn that celebration of a "Combined Rite" is already "the practice" in some places.

43In a lsetter of Msgr. Meeking some movement in the SPCU's position is noted.

Letter of Basil Meeking, Under-Secretary, Secretariat for Promoting Christian Unity to John Hotchkin, Executive Director of the Bishop's Committee for Ecumenical and Interreligious Affairs, NCCB (USA), 22 August 1986, SPCU prot. 4132/86/D. It was the concern of the Secretariat as well as the congregation "not to promote anything which would seem to deny the validity of the baptism of Christians already baptized in their own churches . . . . [This led to the] impression that the proposal [of the combined rite] was an attempt to bring closer together the baptism of those never before baptized and those being received into Catholic communion.

"[As is now clear] the fundamental fact is the widespread and established RCIA programme which both in its catechumenate and in its practice of Christian initiation at Easter grouped together indiscriminately all those to be received into Catholic communion but not needing to be baptized.

"In this case the proposed new rite appears in a different light i.e., as making a distinction which badly needs to be made." The combined rite then is seen as a solution proposed "to remedy a situation that will not otherwise be easily improved." In another (unofficial) letter of Meeking to Hotchkin, 30 October 1986, Meeking states that the Secretariat's objection has been lifted because it was realized that "it is an amelioration of an unsatisfactory situation and not a step in an undesirable direction." The RCIA was confirmed by the Apostolic See in 1988, Letter of Augustin Mayer, Cardinal Prefect, CDW to Archbishop May, President of the NCCB, 19 February 1988, CDW prot. 1192/86. The letter of confirmation notes that the combined rite was "placed in an Appendix by all Conferences that requested [c]onfirmation. The other combined rites were not granted an "unconditional confirmation. Therefore, in order not to delay the granting of confirmation, [they confirmed these sections] conditionally to be placed in an Appendix."

44RCIA, nn. 562–565. The quotations in this section are all from these paragraphs. One can perhaps read between the lines and find an attempt to justify the inclusion of the Rite of Reception into Full Communion at the Easter Vigil. Based on the history of the confirmation (by the Apostolic See) of this particular combined rite recounted above, the inclusion of a "justification" would not be unlikely.

45RCIA, 566 ff.

46OA, 18; RCIA, n. 495. "The celebrant then takes the hands of the newly received person into his own as a sign of friendship and acceptance. With the permission of the Ordinary, another suitable gesture may be substituted, depending on local and other circumstances."

47Cf. *Pontificale Romanum ex decreto Sacrosancti Oecumenici Concilii Vaticani II instauratum auctoritate Pauli PP. VI promulgatum, Ordo confirmationis,* Vatican City 1973. Cf. OICA, pp. 110–11, par. 268. English translation, RCIA, n. 233.

48RCIA, n. 586. This foresees the case of Eastern Christians.

49RCIA, n. 590.

50RCIA, n. 594.

51OA 31.

52Schema 236. Candidate, minister and community have proper parts. *"Deinde veniet ritus ipse: Professio fidei ex parte candidati. Ex parte ministri: oratio cum impositione manuum. Ex parte communitatis: preces gratiarum actionis et deprecationis."*

53Cf. OA, 8, and National Statutes 35.

54OA, 16.

55OA, 17.

56The distinction of Saint-Palais d'Aussac comes to mind: it is less than a confirmation, more than a reconciliation.

57Nor was an imposition of hands mentioned in the Instruction of 20 July 1859.

58Cf. *Lutheran Book of Worship,* Philadelphia 1978, pp. 198–201. This includes a prayer for the gifts of the Holy Spirit with an imposition of hands but no anointing. The liturgy of Holy Baptism (pp. 121–25) also includes such a prayer with an imposition of hands and a consignation (which may include use of oil for anointing).

59See *Pontificium Consilium ad Christianorum Unitatem Fovendam, Directory for the Application of Principles and Norms on Ecumenism,* Vatican City, 25 March 1993, AAS 85 (1993), pp. 1039–1119 (official text is in French). Par. 99a. "There is no doubt about the validity of baptism as conferred in the various Eastern churches. It is enough to establish the fact of the baptism. In these churches the sacrament of confirmation (chrismation) is properly administered by the priest at the same time as baptism. There it often happens that no mention is made of confirmation in the canonical testimony of baptism. This does not give grounds for doubting that this sacrament was also conferred."

60For the Roman Catholic Church's most recent statement on the question of confirmation in the protestant churches, see *Directory for the Application of Principles and Norms on Ecumenism,* 25 March 1993, par. 101. "In the present state of our relations with the ecclesial Communities of the Reformation of the sixteenth century, we have not yet reached agreement about the significance or sacramental nature or even of the administration of the sacrament of Confirmation. Therefore, under present circumstances, persons entering into full communion with the

Catholic church from one of these Communities are to receive the sacrament of Confirmation according to the doctrine and rite of the Catholic church before being admitted to eucharistic communion."

[61]One would see this especially in the Penitential Rite (Scrutiny). The rite should be introduced in such a way that all the participants (candidates, sponsors, catechists, assembly, priests) "hear the comforting message of pardon of sin, for which they will praise the Father's mercy." In some ways, the candidates are signs/symbols of conversion for the faithful.

[62]RCIA, n. 477.

[63]Cf. Schema 276/18, n. 12; Schema 290/18, n. 12. Cf. OA, 18, which drops this reference.

[64]I.e., RCIA, n. 206–43.

[65]I.e., RCIA, n. 487–98.

[66]RCIA, n. 586, 590.

[67]Without going into detail on the problems associated with the sacrament of confirmation and the church's theological understanding of the sacrament, the incongruity noted here seems to pose a problem. Cf. P. Turner, *Confirmation: The Baby in Solomon's Court,* Mahwah, NJ: Paulist Press, 1992, p. 2. "Confirmation is currently being celebrated for many different occasions, according to different models. Confusion exists because these models fight each other against cohesion." Turner treats the Roman Catholic Church's different occasions for celebration of the sacrament of confirmation. He attempts to articulate the problem of the

theological inconsistency associated with confirmation.

[68]I.e., the church should be able to articulate a consistent theology of the sacrament of confirmation, congruent with the various modes of its celebration (with those baptized into the Catholic church as infants, the adult neophytes and validly baptized who are received into full communion).